DEADLY VICES

Deadly Vices

GABRIELE TAYLOR

CLARENDON PRESS · OXFORD

OXFORD
UNIVERSITY PRESS

Great Clarendon Street, Oxford OX2 6DP
Oxford University Press is a department of the University of Oxford.
It furthers the University's objective of excellence in research, scholarship,
and education by publishing worldwide in
Oxford New York

Auckland Cape Town Dar es Salaam Hong Kong Karachi
Kuala Lumpur Madrid Melbourne Mexico City Nairobi
New Delhi Shanghai Taipei Toronto
With offices in
Argentina Austria Brazil Chile Czech Republic France Greece
Guatemala Hungary Italy Japan Poland Portugal Singapore
South Korea Switzerland Thailand Turkey Ukraine Vietnam

Oxford is a registered trademark of Oxford University Press
in the UK and in certain other countries

Published in the United States
by Oxford University Press Inc., New York

British Library Cataloguing in Publication Data
Data available

Library of Congress Cataloging in Publication Data
Taylor, Gabriele.
Deadly vices / Gabriele Taylor.
p. cm.
Includes bibliographical references and index.
ISBN-13: 978–0–19–823580–4 (alk. paper)
ISBN-10: 0–19–823580–1 (alk. paper)
1. Vices. 2. Agent (Philosophy) I. Title.
BJ1534.T39 2006   179′.8—dc22   2006007426

Typeset by Laserwords Private Limited, Chennai, India
Printed in Great Britain
on acid-free paper by
Biddles Ltd., King's Lynn, Norfolk

ISBN 0–19–823580–1   978–0–19–823580–4

1 3 5 7 9 10 8 6 4 2

CONTENTS

ACKNOWLEDGEMENTS

I have greatly benefited from discussions with colleagues and students who during the 1990s attended seminars in which virtues and vices were the principal theme. Versions of some of the material have been published: 'Envy and Jealousy', in *Midwest Studies in Philosophy*, 1988; 'Vices and the Self', in *Philosophy, Psychology and Psychiatry*, 1994; and 'Deadly Vices', in *How Should One Live?*, Oxford University Press, 1966.

Special thanks are owed to Christian Illies for unfailing interest and encouragement, and in particular to Roger Crisp who read and commented most helpfully on some of the chapters.

I INTRODUCTION: VICES AND VIRTUE-THEORY

THE vices to be discussed in this essay are those which in Christian theology were most commonly selected as bringing death to the soul, namely sloth, envy, avarice, pride, anger, lust, and gluttony. My contention is that these so-called 'deadly sins' were correctly so named, and correctly classed together. Irrespective of their theological background they can be seen to be similar in structure in that the agent's thoughts and desires, while differing in content depending on the vice in question, focus primarily on the self and its position in the world. They are similar also in that in each case they are destructive of that self and prevent its flourishing. The exposition of these features will be the main task of the following chapters. If successful, and the vices turn out to be as harmful to their possessor as I take them to be, the conclusions will offer at least negative support for some central claims of an Aristotelean-type virtue-theory. To this extent the present investigation is meant as a contribution to that theory.

It is within a shared framework that the virtues and vices exhibit their opposing features: in both cases it is the agent who is the centre of interest. Vices, like virtues, are qualities of persons and their lives. Virtue-theory is autocentric in its perspective.[1] The agent is seen as concerned with how to conduct her own life, and therefore as approaching ethical questions not as isolated occurrences to be given impartial and universally applicable solutions, but as being embedded in a web of attitudes, interests, and preferences, and as being of urgent importance to herself. Possessing either virtue or

---

[1] The term is John Cottingham's, in 'Partiality and the Virtues', in Roger Crisp (ed.), *How Should One Live? Essays on the Virtues* (Oxford: Oxford University Press, 1996). He thinks that its autocentric orientation is the dominant feature of virtue-theory.

vice consists in the agent being motivated to act in certain patterned ways, in having specific sets of feelings and desires, in taking some but not other factors as relevant considerations in her practical deliberations. This does not mean, however, that the agent envisaged in the theory is doomed to total subjectivity, that what she takes to be a value necessarily is so. There are, on the contrary, standards by reference to which she may, or may fail to, correct her reasoning and attitudes. The fully virtuous comply with this requirement because they get their reasoning right, they possess practical wisdom, a kind of knowledge or sensitivity. Exercising this capacity is of value to them, for the virtues are said to benefit their possessor, to be needed even for leading a flourishing human life. The vices, as their opposites, are then presumably a source of harm to those who possess them.

All these claims are clearly problematic and controversial: what is the relation between agent, virtue, and benefit which supports the apparently implausible view that the virtues at any rate contribute to and possibly are necessary for a person's flourishing? And what are the standards appeal to which should act as a corrective to the agent in her deliberations? Practical reasoning may go wrong in a number of ways. It may be that the agent sees clearly which course of action it would be best to pursue in the circumstances but does not act accordingly. Or she may be wrong or confused in her view as to how much weight should be attached to different reasons for and against the contemplated course of action, or again it may not even occur to her to consider alternatives when she ought to consider them. All of these raise problems. In the first case the agent acts against her own better judgement, and (notoriously) it is hard to see how this can be possible. More directly relevant to the discussion of the vices which is to come are however the latter two alternatives, for the vicious mainly go wrong in these respects. But here the trouble is that what is considered 'beneficial' and what is 'right' and so ought to be done seems to be decided independently of the agent's own views and hence to be imposed upon her. So it would seem that to decide on the correctness or otherwise of an agent's practical reasoning requires some preconceived notion of what is to constitute 'the good life', and this may be thought to be a difficulty for the virtue theorist.

These problems are of course much discussed in the relevant literature[2] though standardly as relating to the virtues only. But since they share the same framework similar difficulties may be expected to arise in connection with a discussion of the vices. The relation between agent, virtue, and benefit or flourishing is paralleled by the relation between agent, vice, and harm or destruction, and appeal is made again to some standard applicable to practical reasoning by means of which harm as well as benefit is to be saved from total subjectivity. What, then, could be the advantage of speaking of the vices rather than the virtues? This approach may seem unhelpfully roundabout, especially as the support it can offer to the claims of virtue-theory is at best only partial, for to show that certain vices are undermining of human flourishing is not by itself to establish that the virtues are needed. Nor does it follow that a person lacking these vices is thereby virtuous in the sense of having a concern for others and acting accordingly. To be without the vices is unlikely to be straightforwardly equivalent to possessing the virtues or to being altruistic.

It may, on the other hand, still be possible to show that being without the vices selected is at least a step towards being receptive to acquiring virtue, and that would be a step in the right direction. But the main advantage of my negative and less ambitious approach lies in this, that it is possible to be much more precise about the nature of the damage inflicted on the agent by some specific vice on the given list than to be about the possible benefit enjoyed by her through possession of a virtue. It is thereby also possible to show that to pronounce them harmful to the agent is not to judge by some externally imposed standard based on what constitutes a good or flourishing human life. The overall assumption underlying the discussion of particular vices I take to be commonplace rather than controversial, namely, that persons wish to lead a life which they perceive as being by and large worthwhile. It is true that judging the practical reasoning of the e.g. envious, proud, or miserly to go wrong

---

[2] See for instance Philippa Foot, 'Virtues and Vices', in *Virtues and Vices* (Oxford: Basil Blackwell, 1978), and *Natural Goodness* (Oxford: Clarendon, 2001), especially ch. 6; Gavin Lawrence, 'The Rationality of Morality' in R. Hursthouse, G. Lawrence, and W. Quinn (eds.), *Virtues and Reasons: Essays in Honour of Philippa Foot* (Oxford: Clarendon, 1995); Crisp, *How Should one Live?* esp. articles by R. Crisp, M. Slote, and B. Hooker; Rosalind Hursthouse, *On Virtue Ethics* (Oxford: Clarendon, 1999), pt. 3.

implies that they are ascribed reasons for taking or avoiding certain courses of action, even though they themselves do not see or agree that they have such reasons. But these reasons are not generated by some standard which may be alien to the agent concerned. On the contrary, the criterion here is internal to their reasoning: given their own aims and points of view they can be shown to be confused. The reasons they are said to have but not to acknowledge are 'internal' reasons in the sense that they have some motive which will be served by acting as this reason directs.[3] They will, of course, also have reasons which explain the point of their ignoring that reason, of disguising its existence from themselves. Sharing the same framework does not mean that the problems arising must be exactly the same whether it is the virtues or the vices that are under discussion. Nor can the practical reasoning of the agent envisaged in the theory be exactly parallel. For example, in *Ethics and the Limits of Philosophy*, Williams speaks of the difficulty which seems to arise when the acquiring or fostering of the virtues is seen as a first-person exercise: it 'has something suspect about it, of priggishness or self-deception' (p. 10). I may, perhaps, keep an eye on myself to make sure that on relevant occasions I act as a generous person would act, and this would seem to make the cultivation of the virtues a rather self-directed and self-centred affair.[4] Williams, however, suggests that to think in these terms is to be not self-directed enough, for to do so is not so much to think about one's actions, or to think about the terms in which one should think about them, it is rather to think about the way in which others might describe the way in which one thinks about one's action. But this line of thought is hardly that of the truly generous. Their thoughts will be engaged with what the other's situation might require them to do, and not with the virtue itself. The virtue-concept is not itself an element of their first-personal deliberations.

In the case of those in the grip of one of the vices it is hardly conceivable that the concept of the vice should itself figure in the

---

[3] So defined by Bernard Williams, 'Internal and External Reasons', *Moral Luck* (Cambridge: Cambridge University Press, 1981).

[4] While such deliberations may always be suspect, the suspicion may not always be justified. See Alan Montefiore, 'Self-Reality, Self-Respect, and Respect for Others', *Midwest Studies in Philosophy* 3 (1978).

person's first-personal reasoning: nobody sets out to cultivate vices of this kind, nobody wants to make sure that she indeed acts as e.g. the envious would act. This is not her aim. Of course, an agent may be self-critical and reflect on the vice in order to see whether she should try and alter the directions of her thought. Introducing the relevant vice-concept into her deliberations would here be a benefit, for it may have the effect of signalling that not all is well with her. But such a person is not in the grip of the vice. There is an asymmetry between the two cases: while the separation of reasoning and virtue-concept seems required if the action is not to be suspect, a similar separation of deliberation and vice-concept rather suggests a lack of awareness, a failure in perception which lends support to the claim that the agent is confused and ignorant.

One task in investigating the vices selected will be to give some content to this notion, to pinpoint the nature and 'object' of the relevant ignorance or types of ignorance, and its resulting harm. 'Object' here refers to both, what the ignorance is of, and what it is for. There must be some point to it, otherwise it would remain inexplicable why the agent should rest apparently content with the kind of confusion which is harmful to her, and why, apparently, she does not recognize this harm. If she is in the grip of one or other of the vices her general attitude to life will be so ingrained that it cannot be explained by reference to the lack of only some one mental state, or the defects of some one mental faculty. Both cognitive and emotional elements are involved. This must be so if individual desires are to be truly embedded in a network of desires, if she truly accepts some reason as a reason for action. Her will, reason, and feeling must be behind it. In the case of the virtuous such cooperation of faculties is thought to be the desired state: there is no struggle between competing inclinations and no struggle between inclination and reason. There is therefore no temptation to stray from the path of virtue, and this in turn indicates that the virtue is well-established.[5] In

---

[5] Aristotle thought that the absence of conflict distinguishes the fully virtuous from the merely continent, for although the latter will be guided by their rational choices they have to struggle in doing so (*Nicomachean Ethics* 1102^{b}26–8), and Aquinas thought of virtues as including the right affective disposition, so that virtuous action is the result of harmonious interaction of the faculties (*Summa Theologiae* (*ST*) 1a2ae qq. 55 art. 4 and 56 art. 6).

the case of the vices such interconnection has the same effect, namely, it guarantees that the relevant vice is firmly established. But here it is a disaster, for it means that the agents concerned are committed to defective modes of perceiving the world and themselves, which will have an impact on their moods, feelings, and desires, and this in turn will confirm the agents' relevant perspective on life. The whole framework of their deliberations is ill-founded, and particular pieces of reasoning are not only affected by the faults of the framework, they also prop it up and nourish it. In this sense it is true of all the vices here considered that what goes wrong with their specific forms of practical reasoning will affect the whole self.

It is tempting, when discussing virtues or vices, to pay special attention to the will. This is so because merely to use the labels 'virtue' and 'vice' indicates candidates for praise or blame, and these are thought inappropriate if the person concerned cannot help herself. There must be some basis for attributing to her at least a degree of control and consequent responsibility. Being concerned with the agent and her way of life it is responsibility for states of mind and character-traits rather than for individual actions which is here in question. Character-traits are complex, interlocking patterns of thought, feeling, desires, and action, and any control a person has over these will certainly be limited, for people are born with different dispositions and temperaments. It is nevertheless also true that to an extent they shape their character, for they are active in discriminating between what is more or less worthwhile and in forming intentions based on such evaluations. This type of control cannot be located in some one faculty; it is not simply an exercise of the will or an act of choice. Since truly accepting a reason for action, and truly committing oneself to some assessment is to incorporate it into the body of one's thought, feelings, and perceptions, the person can be said to give it her assent,[6] or to identify[7] with it, and in doing so to make herself responsible for it.

---

[6] Aquinas, *ST* 2a2ae q. 35 art. 3.

[7] Harry Frankfurt, 'Identification and Wholeheartedness', in Ferdinand Schoeman (ed.), *Responsibility, Character and the Emotions* (Cambridge: Cambridge University Press, 1987).

With so much at stake it is clearly extremely difficult for agents with settled patterns of thoughts, desires, and responses to change their perspective on life. For the characters to be described in the following chapters who are wholly in the grip of some vice it is probably impossible. But of course there are degrees of involvement, a person may be more or less envious, proud, or gluttonous, and of course in any normal person such character-traits are only some of many. It should then be possible, though difficult, to change one's perspective. The repeated efforts involved will be mainly directed towards clarity of thought and a change in the way the world is to be perceived. I can think of no better example than the much-cited case of the mother-in-law, provided by Iris Murdoch. The mother-in-law (M) does not care for her daughter-in-law (D) and thinks her unpolished, pert, and tiresomely juvenile. She may well settle down with a hardened sense of grievance and the confirmed view that her son has married a silly vulgar girl:

However, the M of the example is an intelligent and well-intentioned person, capable of self-criticism, capable of giving careful and just *attention* to an object which confronts her. M tells herself: 'I am old-fashioned and conventional. I may be prejudiced and narrow-minded. I may be snobbish. I am certainly jealous. Let me look again.'   (p. 17, italics in text)[8]

Reflecting about D her vision gradually alters. D is seen to be not vulgar but refreshingly simple, not noisy but gay, not juvenile but youthful. Murdoch's point in telling this story is to direct attention away from action and the will towards the relevance to moral considerations of the introspectable inner life, to illustrate the possibility of taking up a contemplative attitude towards the good. So she assumes that 'M's outward behaviour, beautiful from the start, in no way alters' (p. 18). This is hard to believe. She may not say more or do more for her daughter-in-law, but the warmth she will now be able to infuse into her beautiful politeness will surely affect the manner of what she says and does. It is true, however, that, as Murdoch says, in gradually changing her vision M has been

---

[8] 'The Idea of Perfection' in *The Sovereignty of Good* (London: Routledge and Kegan Paul, 1970).

active, has been doing something which was worth doing in itself, whether or not it affected her behaviour. She did not passively accept her state of mind as something that merely happened to her, but in assessing and attempting to alter it she made it her responsibility. One important consequence, even if her new view of D now exaggerates the daughter-in-law's virtues, is that M herself is better off: she will no longer be a slave to that hardening and crippling sense of grievance. Although this was not M's object, what she has done served her own interest. The conversely contracting and disabling vision of those in the grip of the vices cannot be in their interest; it will on the contrary be instrumental in their lack of flourishing. Since this can hardly be their aim they seem to misconceive deeply their own interests.

It is often remarked by those who these days write about the virtues that the term has fallen out of use, or anyway is not always used to indicate wholly desirable characteristics. It is no longer fashionable to be virtuous, and to be so described often implies not praise but rather the suspicion of a certain primness, or perhaps a more or less self-conscious do-gooding. Similar considerations apply to the use of 'vice'. The 'vices' referred to today tend to be drug-taking, smoking, and drinking rather than the deadly sins. Further, the noun and the adjective have come apart in modern use. Those who take drugs, smoke, or drink are not thought vicious simply because this is what they do. This characterization is chiefly applied to malicious behaviour towards others as exhibited by the cruel or the brutal. It is convenient, however, to use the label to describe those who are in the grip of one or other of the vices selected, and so I shall speak of the envious, proud, etc. as being vicious, even though this may not correspond to common practice. This description refers primarily to the relevant person's (undesirable) state of mind. Not in all cases does viciousness in this sense imply viciousness in the sense of malice or wickedness.

The departure from common practice does not mean, however, that a discussion of individual vices—or for that matter of individual virtues—is of no practical relevance. The vices selected are hardly unknown today. Perhaps they are 'ordinary vices' in being traits which we are not surprised to find in people, at least to some degree.[9] The examination of them here will be restricted to paradigm cases where the salient features of each vice will emerge most clearly. They are therefore extreme cases, where the person is presented as if e.g. pride or envy were her sole characteristic, as if she personified pride or envy. It is in these paradigmatic cases that the vices in question are wholly destructive of the person whose vices they are; that is their nature.

Such concentration on paradigms may seem quite artificial. In normal cases the complexity of a person's character allows other traits to modify or subdue any vicious tendencies so that the agent may suffer no harm, let alone harm of a fundamentally destructive kind, as a result of any of these dispositions. It is possible even that the vice in question itself may modify another harmful trait, and to that extent be useful to its possessor. It is conceivable, for instance, that (vicious) pride may counteract miserliness or cowardice, and on this occasion at least be beneficial. In general the problem is that, assuming the truth of my claim that the paradigm will show the fundamental harm accruing to the vicious, it does not follow from 'repeated exclusive inclinations of a vicious nature are self-destructive in some way' that 'an occasional inclination of this sort is self-destructive in this way'. But if so, then appeal to the paradigm would appear to be irrelevant to those who every now and then tend to act in, say, a miserly or envious fashion. And that in turn might be taken to imply that an investigation of an artificial construct is hardly a worthwhile undertaking.

The various paradigms exhibit excessive viciousness. But if the harm accruing to the agent depends on these paradigms then the question arises whether perhaps it is a consequence not of possessing this or that particular vice, but a consequence rather of the excess. And

---

[9] 'Ordinary vices are the conduct we all expect, nothing spectacular or unusual', Judith N. Shklar, *Ordinary Vices* (Cambridge, Mass.: Harvard University Press, 1984), 1. The vices so labelled are cruelty, hypocrisy, snobbery, betrayal, and misanthropy. These, on the face of it, are very different from the ones here selected, but, as I hope will emerge, some of them at least are not unconnected.

this again might suggest that perhaps any trait if equally dominant and all-embracing would be equally harmful, so that nothing has been shown which is specific to the suggested vices. It would follow that anyone with ordinarily vicious trends need not be at all impressed by the given paradigms, and need not see any appeal to them as providing a reason for trying to suppress or counteract her own vicious tendencies.

The first point in reply to these objections is a concession: features similar to those here ascribed to the vices, such as blindness, lack of sensitivity, faulty practical reasoning, may conceivably apply to some other wholly dominant traits with resulting similar harm to the agent. A fanatic is quite likely to share them—but then it is not clear that a fanatic, because a fanatic, is not thereby also the possessor of this or that deadly vice. But this cannot be true of any trait, and in particular it cannot be true of virtuous ones. Take for example a person who is generous to excess. This means that whenever she sees a person who appears to her in need she will attempt to find a way of giving what is needed, which will be more than or inappropriate to what can rationally be assessed as needed; and further, she will see such need on many more occasions than could be justified from a more detached point of view. Such a person may well come to harm: she may impoverish herself, become a burden to family and friends, be blamed for being unfair on those occasions when it is justice rather than generosity that is required. But this type of harm is only contingent and in certain circumstances perhaps avoidable. She will, however, also misperceive given situations, and so suffer from ignorance and confusion. But these, too, are not altogether of the self-destructive type that befall the vicious. She will escape those because, however misguided, her view is outward-directed, and, though wrong-headed, she has at any rate some appreciation of another's plight.

This at least is the case if we assume her to be really acting from motives of generosity. But there seems to be something inconclusive about her case, something needing explanation. Why does she see the world wholly in terms of needy people making claims on her assistance? This seems sufficiently unbalanced to raise the suspicion that there is some motivation behind this world-view, so that more is at stake than straightforward generosity. Maybe she wishes to see herself as a saintly servant of mankind. But if so then she does not think and act as a truly generous person would think and act. Maybe she simply gives in to those warm feelings she has towards people. But here, too, virtue and excess are mutually exclusive. The truly generous person gives more thought to the situation confronting her, and her reactions are accordingly more differentiated. This point has some support in the way we think of the virtues and vices respectively: while we may be in the grip of, say, avarice or envy, we do not think of a person as being in the grip of e.g. generosity or honesty, courage or justice. 'Being in the grip of' implies being subject to strong feelings which overwhelm the agent and leave her without control. This is not the picture we have of those possessing the virtues. It is precisely because they are not wholly in the power of such feelings that their practical reasoning does not go similarly astray.

I conclude that even if it is not necessarily only the vicious who suffer destructive self-harm, the traits which lead to such harm are certainly limited. But the problem concerning the relation between paradigm and ordinary vices remains unanswered. That is, supposing it to be correct that being in the total grip of a vice is destructive of the agent, what if anything follows for the ordinary person who every now and then is tempted by miserly, envious, etc. considerations, and acts accordingly? Like the 'excessively generous' this person, too, may come to harm. Acting in a miserly fashion, for instance, she may lose her friends. But such contingencies depending on individual circumstances are again not to the point, the only harm in question being of a self-destructive kind, and for the ordinary person this is unlikely to occur. But the question of motivation arises in this case as well. How do we know that she thought and acted as a miser would? Judging by her behaviour alone does not supply the answer, for there may be alternative explanations of why she acted as she did. In, say, not having valid reasons for holding on to the money urgently needed by a relative on medical grounds she may be merely mean rather than miserly.[10] For her action to have been vicious she had to act from the relevant disposition. If so, then there is in her a vicious disposition which in her case, not being prominent and usually counteracted

---

[10] This distinction is relevant to the case of the miser, discussed in Ch. 3.

by other traits, may well be relatively harmless. But even if she acts viciously only occasionally she will have a share, if only a small one, of the excess exhibited by the paradigm. Given the vice is as described, 'having a share of its excess' means being at least at the threshold of some potentially harmful state of ignorance and confusion. Consideration of the paradigm would enable her to see more clearly what that harm consists in. It would thereby give her reason to make sure that the disposition remains under check, reason to be aware of such a tendency and to take care that it does not grow and gradually become more prominent. For if not kept under guard it may become uncontrolled and uncontrollable, the first step on a slippery slope.

The link between excess and the vices is hardly surprising: if the virtuous are balanced in their judgements then the vicious, by contrast, will lack such balance and to that extent lack control over their feelings; if the virtuous have whatever feelings and attitudes are appropriate on the relevant occasions then those of the vicious will be inappropriate in ways which can be summarized as 'excessive'. By the same token, if possessing the virtues in some way benefits their possessor, then the possession of the vices is likely to harm those who exercise them. The examination of individual vices to come can be seen as a detailed account of the form of excess resulting in specific harm to which a particular vicious disposition is prone.

The discussions to follow will, then, concentrate on the essence of each vice, and treat their possessors as personifications. They will show a structural resemblance to each other, but there is no suggestion that all vices are of that type. There seems no reason to suppose that there must be one and only one structure appeal to which will explain and justify labelling certain traits as 'vicious', just as there need be no one structure to which all the 'virtuous' have to conform. Other vices may however be consequent on the possession of one or the other of the present set: the deadly sins were also thought to be 'capital sins', the source of further vicious dispositions. This suggestion will be examined in a later chapter. But the discussions to follow cannot be seen as an attempt to give a uniform account of all possible vices. Similarly, but on a larger scale, in offering a defence of certain aspects of virtue-theory I do not wish to imply that in virtue-theory alone are to be found the answers to all the questions raised in moral philosophy.

2 'DEADLY SINS'

THE lists of the vices traditionally labelled 'deadly sins' normally cite seven in number, and normally comprise sloth (*acedia* or accidie), pride, envy, covetousness, lust, gluttony, and anger or wrath. Their overall defect was said to consist in inadequate control of reason over the passions,[1] and the 'passions', in one form or another, seem indeed to be essentially constitutive of these vices. Some—pride, envy, and anger—share their names with those of emotions; others—lust and gluttony—seem crucially concerned with indulgence in pleasure; sloth similarly involves a form of self-indulgence, and covetousness implies limitless desire. The passions, therefore, suggest themselves as a suitable starting-point for a discussion of these vices. Since however 'passion' has been used indiscriminately to cover whatever was deemed not to be within the realm of 'reason', it is clearly necessary to draw further distinctions and discuss different phenomena as the need arises. I shall begin with some remarks about the nature of emotions and moods.

Intuitively it is quite plausible to think of emotions as threats to rationality. Certainly, when in the grip of an emotion such as anger or fear we do not see clearly and may well act in ways we later regret. Nonetheless, emotions are not merely passions which befall us, in their passivity to be sharply distinguished from active reason. They involve different ways of assessing the world, and this in turn requires that there be some cognitive element in the complex which makes up the emotional state. The fear of the dog is likely to be based on the thought that it might bite, anger at some remark on the belief

---

[1] E.g. Thomas Aquinas, *Summa Theologiae* (*ST*) 1a2ae q. 71, art. 2: 'man derives his species from his rational soul: and consequently whatever is contrary to the order of reason is, properly speaking, contrary to the nature of man, as man. Therefore ... vice is contrary to man's nature, insofar as it is contrary to reason.'

that it was insulting. Emotions have intentional content: they have an 'internal object', constitutive of the emotion, which is expressed in propositions stating the agent's view of the given situation. To experience fearful suspicion, for example, is to feel anxious at the believed or imagined fact that some harm is about to befall one. Its intentional content makes an emotion the emotion it is, and serves to distinguish one from the other. Emotions also have 'external objects' in the sense that they are directed towards a specific thing or state of affairs. They have a focus, which may be actually in the world or believed to be in the world (the dog, the insulting remark) but may also be merely a piece of fantasy. (You may frighten yourself by telling yourself a ghost story.)[2] Since 'internal objects' are, and 'external objects' are not, constitutive of the emotion itself it is clearly possible for an emotional state to have the former but lack the latter object. This is so in those states which are commonly labelled 'moods'. While moods must have an intentional content to be identified as this or that particular mood, they lack an 'external object' in the sense of lacking a focus for their reaction which can be identified independently of the emotional state itself, and which is to an extent explanatory of it. Thus a lost job may be that which a person is depressed about and reference to which explains her state. But as a mood depression is not 'about' any aspect of life in particular, and no particular event can be picked out as its explanation. The distinction between emotion and mood is obscured if the two senses of 'object' are not sufficiently disentangled. Anthony Kenny, for instance, after explaining that the difference between sensations and emotions consists in the latter's being essentially directed towards objects, asks whether there are not objectless emotions, such as pointless depression? The answer he gives is that pointless depression is not objectless depression, for the objects of depression are the things which seem black.[3] But this is a mistake if, as his remark about the distinction between sensations and emotions seems to imply, he is thinking of external objects: the 'black things' are not the focus of the person's depression, that which it is directed towards. Rather, 'seeing everything as black' is at least

<hr />

[2] Patricia Greenspan discusses in detail the notions of 'internal' and 'external' objects in *Emotions and Reason* (New York: Routledge, 1988).

[3] In *Action, Emotion and Will* (London: Routledge and Kegan Paul, 1963), 60–1.

a partial description of what depression amounts to, and so, unlike the lost job, not an independently identifiable object or situation. It is the internal, not the external, object. By contrast, the distinction between sensations on the one hand, and emotions or moods on the other, is that, unlike the other two, sensations have no intentional content and so do not have an object in either sense.

In the case of emotions we can distinguish between occurrent states and dispositions: to be in an occurrent emotional state is actually to experience the emotion, so to be in the state of fear-of-that-dog is to feel like running away now. But I may be afraid of the dog and yet for long periods feel no fear at all. The emotion is dispositional in that I am disposed to experience it in specific circumstances, when walking past the dog-owner's house, seeing the dog in the distance, etc. A somewhat similar distinction may be drawn in the case of moods, though since these lack external objects it cannot be explained in terms of the perception or recollection of or association with that type of object. Moods may be occurrent or standing:[4] to be in an occurrent mood, or mood-state, is to see the world in the relevant way and to have the experience of so seeing it. Occurrent moods therefore have two elements: a form of awareness, or manner of perceiving the world, and an experienced consciousness of this awareness, which may be any one (or possibly more) of a cluster of appropriate feelings. If in depression the mode of awareness may be described as seeing things in the world as uniformly black, then the experienced consciousness of this may be hopelessness, despair, weariness, or perhaps indifference. Such occurrent moods are changeable and may be short-lived; some external event may change an elated mood into a depressed one, or the other way about. 'Standing mood', or 'frame of mind', refers to the form of awareness only. This may live and die with the person's experience of it, in which case the distinction is wholly theoretical. But it may also outlast it. A person's mode of perceiving the world may be elated or depressed without her constantly so experiencing it. A standing mood is compatible with a range of occurrent moods (the standing mood of depression is compatible with the occurrent mood of despair or the occurrent mood of indifference, etc.) and

---

[4] Claire Armon-Jones introduces and discusses these distinctions in *Varieties of Affect* (London: Harvester Wheatsheaf, 1991).

it is also possible with contrasting emotional states: although in a happy (standing) mood a person may feel temporarily miserable about some adverse happening, and a (standing) mood of depression may not be so severe as to exclude occasional feelings of hope or pleasure.

A standing mood or frame of mind which is long-lasting may be called an attitude, and if that attitude is dominant in a person's life in that it is fairly constant and has a tendency to govern a high proportion of her moods, emotions, and behaviour, then it is a personality-trait. Descriptions such as 'a jovial man', 'a nervous, timid girl' pick out different attitudes towards the world and other people, as well as the corresponding behaviour-patterns and reactions. A personality-trait may or may not be seen as a character-trait. If thought of as traits of personality they are normally regarded as being genetically and environmentally determined, and so by themselves not proper objects of praise or blame, though of course they may endear or repel. If thought of as traits of character, on the other hand, they tend to be seen as something for which the person concerned is at least partially responsible, the idea being that normally we can do something about what we are given, that we need not be wholly in the grip of what dispositions we may find within ourselves. Indeed, to 'find' them, to achieve some clarity about their nature, is a first step towards gaining a degree of control. To a large extent the development from childhood to mature adulthood seems to consist in learning how to handle such dispositions.

The vices to be discussed, being 'sins' and so something regarded as blameworthy, are all to be thought of as character-traits, so that the preceding analysis is, in different ways, relevant to all of them. In this chapter I shall illustrate the application of the analysis with reference to the particular vice of *acedia* or sloth. Sloth has features which can be seen to be clearly analogous to those of the other vices to be discussed. On the other hand, it also has characteristics which set it apart from them. (In Dante's *Purgatory* it is the only one of the sins falling into the category of 'defective love'.) In using it as an illustration it will therefore fulfil the function of bringing out those aspects in which the vices selected can be expected to be similar, while also emphasising some points of difference.

The labels 'sloth' and 'slothful' are rarely used these days to refer to some person's state or character-trait. Originally, in its theological context, 'sloth' or *acedia* indicated a very specific state of psychic exhaustion and general listlessness to which, owing to the conditions of their lives, the Egyptian desert monks were thought to be particularly prone. To them it was the most dangerous and oppressive of temptations.[5] In the course of the Middle Ages the understanding of the sin broadened, and from being a kind of depression and boredom with the monastic form of life specifically it became a moral perversion which might be manifested by anybody. For Aquinas it is a universal form of moral misconduct, an aversion of the appetite from its own good because of the bodily hardships that accompany its attainment (*Summa Theologiae* (*ST*) 2a2ae q. 35). The treatment of *acedia* by the scholastics naturally differed from that which it received in more popular literature, designed to give practical and concrete advice. Their authors therefore tended to look not so much at the relevant states of mind as at their behavioural manifestations. The slothful neglect their religious duties, they do not say their prayers, they sleep through the sermon. Those suffering from it are to learn to be patient, and in particular they are to work hard. Scholastics, on the other hand, concentrated on the mental aspect of the sin, on the state of the person's soul or mind. It is possible, after all, for someone to be outwardly punctilious in performing his duties but to do so in the wrong spirit, without joy, for example, or beset by doubt. Sloth, therefore, spans a wide range of both behavioural and mental phenomena. Among the most commonly mentioned are laziness, idleness, complacency, irresponsibility, boredom, restlessness of body, melancholy, and despair.

Today, if we think in these terms at all, we tend to think of the slothful as being generally inactive, indolent, and lazy. That is, we tend to pick out the behavioural manifestations of the vice. Accordingly, it is sometimes thought absurd to regard it as in any way a deadly sin. So for example Evelyn Waugh remarks: 'The word "Sloth" is seldom on modern lips. When used, it is a mildly

---

[5] The history of the concept is explained by S. Wenzel, *The Sin of Sloth: Acedia in Medieval Thought and Literature* (Chapel Hill: University of North Carolina, 1967).

facetious variant of "indolence", and indolence, surely, so far from being a deadly sin, is one of the most amiable of weaknesses. Most of the world's troubles seem to come from people who are too busy.'[6] Perhaps so, but this only suggests that such 'amiable weakness' cannot be all that was thought to be involved in the possession of the sin.

My proposal was to examine sloth not only from the point of view of its deadliness, but also to illustrate the relevance of the discussion of emotional states to the case of the various vices. Maybe this, too, is ill-conceived:

Medieval moral psychologists analysed accidie in detail, since for many it was not just the major spiritual failing to which those who should have been dutiful succumbed, but to feel it at all was a sin. By the fifteenth century the popular conception of 'the sin of sloth' had ceased to be a state of mind and had shifted to manifest behaviour (or the lack of it). 'Sloth' had taken on its modern connotation.

I offer accidie as an example of an obsolete emotion, since I think modern people do not associate any specific emotion with laziness or procrastination in the carrying out of tasks that duty demands.[7]

It is quite true that we do not think that there is some one emotion the occurrence of which results in inaction when we ought to act, and maybe even medieval moral psychologists did not believe precisely this. It does not follow, however, that 'sloth' may not indicate a state of mind, or indeed an emotional state of mind. Behaviour by itself can hardly be a reliable indicator of the vice, for what is seen as laziness or procrastination may not be due to sloth, and conversely, sloth may not express itself in these forms of behaviour. It is not an occurrent emotion but a standing mood which is here relevant: the slothful are in a specific frame of mind, they take a certain view of the world. But a long-term, well-established perspective on life may find expression in all sorts of different occurrent states and types of behaviour. We therefore, in medieval literature, find lists of a variety of behaviour and mental states under the heading of *acedia*. Sloth is a complex phenomenon, and different elements need to be

---

[6] In *The Seven Deadly Sins* (London: Sunday Times Publications, 1962), 57–64. Waugh himself sees sloth, or something very like it, prevalent in various areas of modern life.

[7] Rom Harré, *Personal Being* (Oxford: Basil Blackwell, 1983), 128.

sorted out to show why it is by no means absurd to regard it as deadly.

Indolence is no doubt a typical characteristic of the slothful. The possibly most indolent character in literature is in precisely this state:

Oblomov began thinking. But he could not make up his mind what he was to think of first: the bailiff's letter, or moving out of the flat, or looking through the accounts. He was lost in a flood of wordly cares, and remained lying in bed, turning over from side to side. At times sudden cries were heard in the room: 'oh dear, oh dear! You can't run away from life—it gets at you everywhere.'[8]

Indolence may of course be merely a passing occurrent mood, which may be experienced as pleasant or unpleasant. The temporarily indolent may feel pleasantly lazy and relaxed, believing possibly that as it happens there is at present no effort required of them and they may as well take it easy. They may also feel unpleasantly heavy and inert, and perhaps guilty in not doing what they think they ought. And there is a possible range of feelings in between these two extremes. But whatever the person's experience, if such states are short-lived and infrequent they are unlikely to do much harm, and may on the contrary be a healthy state which it is good to experience every now and then. The indolence of the slothful is frequent and long-lasting. Oblomov's inclination to stay in bed is his response not merely to troublesome demands of everyday life, but also to friends' invitations to various entertainments. Social life seems to have as little attraction for him as does organizing his household or going to work.

Originally, *acedia* very specifically referred to indolence which resulted in neglect of religious duties; later it was taken to cover indolence with respect to any duties. There are two implications here: first, both interpretations imply what might be called an 'external' view of how human beings ought to conduct their lives. They ought to meet this or that obligation, fulfil this or that duty. Failure in this respect is to be sinful, or anyway morally defective. The implication is that there is some objective moral standard according to which human behaviour and attitudes are to be judged. But reference to such a standard does not necessarily help to show why the possession

---

[8] Ivan Goncharov, *Oblomov* (Harmondsworth: Penguin, 1983), 24.

of a 'deadly sin' should be so disastrous for its owner. No doubt there are inconveniences attached to ignoring established moral rules, but there may be ways of avoiding or minimizing these. To feel the discomforts of guilt or shame the agent concerned has to internalize such rules, and if she wholeheartedly accepts them then any breach of them will bring her unease, whether or not they are generally accepted rules. It is no external standard but a person's mode of awareness which is relevant to the case of harmful indolence.

Secondly, and relatedly, the crucial form of indolence was taken to refer to a certain area of life only, namely the neglect of duties. But this seems too narrow a view. Suppose Oblomov neglected whatever duties he might be said to have, but spent much time and energy in the pursuit of other activities. He was keen on sport, say, or on the arts, or social intercourse, and his duties were neglected so that he might have more time for the enjoyment of these. Given the chaotic circumstances of his life this may be imprudent and weak, but however the morality of such a life might be evaluated, he could hardly be said to suffer from indolence. His problem is that none of these activities arouses his interest or stimulates his energies, either.

An Oblomov-type indolence may take various forms: the person concerned may see that there are things worth doing and achieving in life, if only he could make the requisite effort. Alternatively, as far as he can see there is nothing on offer worth making an effort for, and so he remains inert; or possibly his view may shift between these two, or remain ambiguous. Although the initial mode of awareness may be different in these cases, the agents' ultimate view of themselves and of the world will be the same.

To believe that there is a concrete possibility of achieving something very worthwhile and yet to take no steps towards this goal might be a case of weakness of will. The agent concerned has conflicting reasons for acting. On the one hand she believes that engaging in a certain activity would be enjoyable, prudent, or fulfilling, on the other she sees that not doing so would lead to greater ease and comfort. She thinks the first reason the weightier, but acts on the second. This appears to correspond to Aquinas's model: a rational approach to the situation is overridden by the (non-rational) desire for ease. In her own view she ought to have acted otherwise. If so, familiar problems about weakness of will appear: how could she sincerely believe that she ought to act and yet not do so? Moreover, particularly if the situation is a recurrent one it is unlikely that she will achieve the ease and comfort she had in view; she is likely to despise herself for her weakness. If the situation is a recurrent one then there is reason to suspect that she cannot believe sincerely in the worthwhileness of the rejected course of action. Perhaps what the agent expressed as a sincere belief was no more than a wishful thought that the world be different, a piece of fantasy which would not constitute a reason for action. It is however possible that the agent does sincerely believe that she should take one course of action and yet embark on another. There are types and, within these types, degrees of sincerity. There is what may be called 'intellectual' or 'theoretical' sincerity: an agent may see clearly that a certain course of action may for some reason be more worthwhile than any others that might be open to her, but see equally clearly that she is not prepared, for some reason, ever to set out to achieve the relevant aim. The 'should' in 'I should do this' is meant as 'ideally, this is what I should do'. Oblomov occasionally exhibits this type of sincerity, when he can see that there would be rewards for bestirring himself, but also knows, regretfully, that this prospect is not enough for him to make the effort.

In such a case, since the agent does not seriously consider taking the relevant course of action, she cannot be said to be properly engaged in practical reasoning at all, for she knows, or half-knows, that the conclusion she will reach will not influence what she decides and does. Within the area of practical reasoning there are degrees of sincerity. At one extreme is the 'shallowly sincere'[9] who, perhaps under pressure of temporary strong feelings, means what she says at the time of saying it, but her conviction is short-lived. The 'wholeheartedly sincere', on the other hand, will have incorporated their stated belief into the body of their thoughts, feelings, and desires. If an agent is merely shallowly sincere then her practical reasoning is wholly ineffective, and, if the pattern is frequently repeated, is self-deceptive. She does not really accept that the contemplated course of action is more worthwhile than is her ease and comfort. The persistently shallowly sincere do not in their perspective on life differ fundamentally from those who on all

---

[9] The terminology is Fingarette's in *Self-Deception* (London: Routledge and Kegan Paul, 1977), 51–2.

or most relevant occasions deny that reasons for positive action are overriding, and undisguisedly subscribe to the view that it is usually or always better to do nothing. This last character may think, like the theoretically sincere, that there are worthwhile things to be achieved in life, but also think the required effort too great. Alternatively, she may think that there is nothing in life worth making an effort for.

These two attitudes indicate two distinguishable but interlocking standing moods, that of indolence and that of boredom. The indolent see the world in terms of making demands which they think too hard to fulfil, they will not, or think they cannot, make the requisite effort. The bored focus on what seems to them the lack of attraction in any possible course of action. These moods interconnect: the bored are likely to be also indolent. The converse case is not quite so straightforward since the indolent may not always feel their indolence; that is, they may amuse themselves quite well with entertaining fantasies. There are stretches of time when Oblomov, lying on his bed, lets his imagination roam pleasantly. At such times he is not bored. However, these are only relatively short spells, and it is highly improbable that anyone can be entrenched in a life of total indolence and never have the emotional experience of it. Engaging in a fantasy-life would rather seem to be a means of escaping from that experience. There will then at least be periods when the indolent will also be bored. They share the burden of inertia since for neither of them is there anything in the world worth making an effort for. So they do not engage with the world, and such lack of engagement is a central feature of boredom.

Boredom may be an emotional state; that is, have both an intentional content and an 'external' object which is the focus of the 'internal' one. We may be bored by a book, a conversation, the job in hand. There is a distinction to be drawn here, from the agent's point of view: she may think e.g. the job a boring one and yet not be bored. This may be because she decides to make it more interesting to herself, carry it out with meticulous care, or look for possible improvements. Alternatively, she may accept the boringness of the job and let her thoughts be engaged with other things to make time pass more pleasantly. In that case, although bored by the job, she is not bored, and if she is good at distracting her thoughts she may not mind, or may even seek, work which is inherently uninteresting. Either alternative offers an escape from a mental condition which is unpleasant and makes time hang heavy on one's hands. When being bored by e.g. the job, that which is supposed to occupy one's time constructively fails to do so, while also preventing us from making better use of it. As in the case of indolence, relatively short and infrequent periods of boredom are unlikely to do any harm to anybody. Never feeling bored may even be a defect, for the attempt to inject interest and the ability to distract one's thoughts may be used to conceal from oneself the reality of the situation. Bernard Williams remarks that there is in life such a thing as justified boredom:

Thus ... someone who was, or who thought himself, devoted to the radical cause might eventually admit to himself that he found a lot of its rhetoric excruciatingly boring. He might think that he ought not to feel that, that the reaction was wrong, and merely represented an unworthiness of his ... However, he might rather feel that it would not necessarily be a better world in which no-one was bored by such rhetoric and that boredom was, indeed, a perfectly worthy reaction.[10]

It is the emotional state of boredom which may sometimes be justified and may lead the person concerned to change her views and way of life in certain respects. The mood of boredom cannot be justified in this manner, for there is no specifiable 'object' the nature of which is rightly seen by the agent as making it not worth engaging with. For the same reason ways of escape which are possible when in the emotional state are now blocked: there can be no diverting thoughts because all thoughts will now be gloomy. Nor can steps be taken to avoid the boring situation, as the uninteresting job could conceivably be dropped. The mood of boredom is therefore inherently more serious than is the emotion. No escape offers itself. Things in the world seem undifferentiated, they are uniform in their unattractiveness, so there is nothing to take an interest in, and consequently nothing to motivate one to act. Since nothing seems worthwhile one may as well do what requires least effort, or requires no effort at all. Naturally, the bored are also indolent.

The state of boredom is unpleasant enough when a temporary experience only. It is harmful when the mood is the overall standing

---

[10] 'The Macropulos Case', in *Problems of the Self* (Cambridge: Cambridge University Press, 1973), 95.

one. It is a bleak mode of perception. The world is uniformly uninteresting, and since therefore the person sees nothing to engage with, she is herself thoroughly uninteresting to herself. Neither world nor self is worth taking trouble over. Being bored with oneself makes indolence inevitable; it is an aspect of that boredom.

Consciousness of the standing mood of boredom may take the form of a range of possible occurrent moods, of which one or the other may predominate. The occurrent mood may be boredom itself, the state where time seems to stand still and to present the problem of having to be filled. But empty time is monotonous and does not encourage any specific response. ' "Always the same thing—how boring!" said Oblomov with a yawn' (*Oblomov*, p. 27). Schopenhauer thinks that 'only those who have been handed over to boredom are not pressed and plagued by time'.[11] It is true that those who are bored are not always trying to catch up with time, are not always worried that there might not be time to do this or that. But for them time is a pressure in a different, possibly more literal sense: it is a burden which oppresses them. Time is a drag, an obstacle to be got rid of, to be somehow killed. It is a pressure in its very emptiness, lacking anything which could make one feel alive. There is nothing to do in that time, and so the heaviness is in oneself. Perceiving time as empty is to feel oneself a burden to oneself.

Consciousness of this burden is characteristic of the mood of indolence, and is what distinguishes it from mere idleness. Such consciousness is of both mental and physical inactivity. Not seeing the world as something to be acted upon is also to see one's own body as inert and to feel it as a useless weight.[12] Consciousness of this type is incompatible with any feeling of pleasure or joy, so that the mood of indolence is closely connected with states of joylessness and depression. Once these moods have a grip, states of hopelessness and despair, or alternatively states of fatigue and weariness, are a natural consequence. The standing mood of boredom can therefore be seen to be responsible for a range of phenomena traditionally listed as manifestations of sloth.

[11] A. Schopenhauer, *Parerga and Paralipomena*, ii. ch. 12, para. 151.
[12] This state is well described by John Casey in *Pagan Virtue* (Oxford: Oxford University Press, 1992).

I have spoken of the standing moods of indolence and boredom as distinguishable but interlocking. The characterization of the slothful may take as its starting-point either of these moods; the end-result will be the same. This is so because the difference between them consists in merely a change of focus, respectively a view of the world as not worth engaging with, and a view of the agent as not prepared to make the effort necessary for engagement. According to which view predominates there will be further differences in their outlook. Perhaps, if the mood is boredom, they will tend to blame the world rather than themselves for this deplorable state of affairs, and conversely, perhaps, if the mood is indolence. But in their lack of engagement both exhibit the fundamental feature of sloth. Their occurrent moods and emotional states may vary, but they will always be of the negative, depressive kind, and so tend to reinforce their boredom and indolence. Behaviourally their frames and states of mind are likely to be those of a lazy, idle, and withdrawn person. But this is not so necessarily. Among the possible characteristics of the slothful mentioned on medieval lists is that of restlessness, and the restless are not only active, they are feverishly so. Here we seem to have a case which contradicts the basic characterization given.

But there are different views on the nature and implication of 'activity' which need disentangling. Kant thinks of activity as the sustenance of life: 'It is by his activities and not by enjoyment that man feels that he is alive. The busier we are the more we feel that we live and the more conscious we are of life. In idleness we not only feel that life is fleeting but we also feel lifeless.'[13] The opposite opinion is expressed by the aestheticist in Kierkegaard's *Either/Or*. He thinks of activity as being a kind of restlessness which is incompatible with the spiritual life, and consequently he considers idleness a good rather than an evil, and being active not at all a desirable state. According to him it is enjoyment and not activity with which we should fill our lives.[14] Clearly, we have here two quite different views as to how 'activity' is to be understood. For Kant, 'being active' implies a

---

[13] Immanuel Kant, *Lectures on Ethics*, 'Occupation', tr. Louis Infield (London: Methuen, 1970).

[14] Søren Kierkegaard, *Either/Or*, i. *The Rotation Method*, tr. D. F. Swenson and L. Marvin Swenson (Princeton, NJ: Princeton University Press, 1971), 284–5.

wholehearted and rationally justified commitment on the part of the agent. He is engaged with what he thinks worthwhile and is right in thinking so. The aestheticist, on the other hand, has in mind a 'being busy', a form of being active which lacks the implication of fully engaging the agent and being worth the effort expanded on it. It is busyness and not activity which may be sharply contrasted with enjoyment, and it is activity and not busyness which is incompatible with boredom and indolence. Keeping oneself busy may be a means towards finding an activity which holds one's interest and affords a way of escaping from boredom. But it may also be a means of trying to disguise from oneself one's own negative state.

Escape through busyness is a familiar phenomenon, often discussed particularly in relation to the housewife's lot. Betty Friedan, for instance, reporting the results of her questionnaire answered by graduate housewives in the 1950s, notices:[15] 'They were so *busy*—busy shopping, chauffeuring, using their dishwashers and dryers and electric mixers, busy gardening, waxing, polishing, helping with the children's homework . . .' (p. 208). But busyness, though it may temporarily disguise, does not alter the basic frame of mind of boredom, for there still is, in the (honest) agent's view, nothing in her life worth making all that effort for: ' "It's as if there is nothing I really have to do, though there is plenty to do around the house. So I keep a bottle of martinis in the refrigerator, and I pour myself some so I'll feel more like doing something" ' (p. 221). Busyness, unlike activity, tends to be accompanied by fatigue and weariness. Kant was wrong to oppose enjoyment to activity, for the interest and involvement implied by 'being active' are themselves a form of enjoyment, and there will also be the pleasure of feeling alive in the consciousness of doing something with one's time. But the contrast Kant had in mind was a life full of activities as opposed to a life devoted to pleasures (*Genuss*), for he goes on: 'The pleasures of life do not fill time full, but leave it empty . . . The present may, indeed, seem full to us, but if we have filled it with play, etc., the appearance of fullness will be confined to the present. Memory will find it empty.'

---

[15] *The Feminine Mystique* (Harmondsworth: Pelican, 1982), ch. 10: 'Housewifery expands to fill the time available.'

Kant here makes two points: first, in his view indulgence in pleasures cannot command the kind of commitment which is needed to avoid boredom and fatigue and make one feel alive. Secondly, at times mere busyness may appear as activity to the person concerned, but when thinking about this time it will reveal its emptiness. The points are connected, but only the second is relevant to the present context. The first, if true, will link the slothful with the gluttonous and the lustful, and will be discussed later (Ch. 6). Kant's second point implies the claim that temporary engagement with what one is doing is not sufficient for activity if it does not, so to speak, pass the test of time. The engagement, though momentarily satisfying, will not last; it will not keep the person occupied, nor will it generate other fields of interest. It is a wholly superficial engagement, and indeed reveals aspects of the shallowly sincere. The criterion for its superficiality may but need not be as Kant suggests, the agent's own realization of its barrenness. For this it does not really matter what it is that fills the time. Rather, what is important is how the agent views this content. Querry, the central character in Graham Greene's *A Burnt-Out Case*, is an eminent architect and would hardly be described as filling his time with play. Yet he reveals himself as being slothful: in reply to the question whether there is anything he wants he says 'Nothing. I want nothing.' And nearly adds 'that is my trouble'. And also: 'I suffer from nothing. I no longer know what suffering is. I have come to an end of all that too.'[16] But not everyone is as self-analytical as is Querry, and in other cases the shallowness of the engagement will show itself in its lack of being goal-directed. Activities generate reasons for further activities, but where the interest is temporary and superficial it does not lead anywhere. Activity has a coherence which busyness lacks. Oblomov would here again be an example, when at some period of his life he fancies himself in love with Olga and is bullied by her into bursts of non-idleness. But these lead nowhere and do nothing to cure his indolence.

It is natural that the bored, confronted by empty time, should try and busy themselves, if not with the view of trying genuinely to improve their situation then to create the illusion that their lives are

---

[16] Evelyn Waugh, in *Seven Deadly Sins*, speaks of Querry as the representation of the depth of sloth.

after all not meaningless and they need not despair. They have an interest in deceiving themselves. The range of possible time-fillers is wide: the good-natured, like Oblomov, may simply try to please others. Some, like Querry, may try charitable work. Others may tend to be destructive and cruel, possibly to find something to interest and gratify, possibly to vent their frustration. Ibsen's Hedda Gabler may here be an example. The illusion may or may not be successful, and the response to failure very different. Oblomov soon sinks again into what appears to be fairly contented apathy. Hedda Gabler shoots herself. She acts consistently enough, for seeing no point in her existence, she puts an end to it. The case of Oblomov, however, presents a problem. Surrounded by devoted and loyal friends his financial and household problems are solved, he need not bestir himself and can stay in bed as long as he likes. He is not busy, let alone active, and yet not on the whole dissatisfied. Only sometimes occurs to him the vague thought that he might have done better things in life. He is not usually conscious of himself as a burden to himself. But sloth was to be found in the person's view of life and consequent explicit or disguised depressed state of mind. By this criterion Oblomov seems to escape sloth. But on the other hand, he also appears to be the very paradigm case of slothfulness. How is this paradox to be explained?

Sloth has so far been characterized in terms of boredom and indolence. To be in a slothful mood is to be in a state of which the interrelated components are feelings of physical and mental inertness and a cognitive appraisal of the world as not worth engaging with. The slothful, then, are inclined to be in that state. But sloth is to be thought of as a vice, not as merely a pathological state due to natural dispositions from which some unfortunates have to suffer. The slothful are to be seen as having some responsibility for their condition. Aquinas, in reply to the objection that sloth cannot be a mortal sin since even the virtuous may suffer from it, explains that there may be an inclination towards this state in even holy men, but they are not therefore sinful because they withhold rational assent.[17] The implication is that the sinfully slothful do assent to being as they are. In assenting they have exercised their will and so can be held responsible.

---

[17] *ST* 2a2ae q. 35 art. 3.

From this point of view Oblomov is viciously slothful because he has assented to his state. As was pointed out in the last chapter, this does of course not mean that by some act of will he could have changed his moods and way of perceiving the world. One cannot all at once achieve a difference in one's outlook. He assented rather in the sense that he made no attempt at all to view critically his way of life and mode of awareness, that he gave no serious thoughts to possible alternatives but indulged merely in idle imaginings which disguised rather than highlighted his attitude towards the world and himself. Consequently, he never tried to modify in any way his states of mind but allowed them to become established. It is in this sense that the slothful can be said to be responsible for their state: they are not merely inclined to be in moods of boredom and indolence, they do not even in thought oppose such inclinations, and by making no attempt to alter their vision of the world let themselves slide into those occurrent moods which result from a frame of mind that sees no effort as worthwhile. Oblomov's relative state of satisfaction towards the end of his life is, then, not a relevant consideration; it does, on the contrary, indicate his final resignation to his condition, his fully assenting to it.

This, however, does not answer the question of why an Oblomov-type state should be regarded as vicious, of why assenting to it should be so bad. Aquinas, of course, offered an objective framework yielding objective criteria for how life ought to be lived, and in judging Oblomov to be viciously slothful some external standard appears to be appealed to. But the assumptions here are only the minimal ones, that as persons we are agents capable of leading a life, and that individual agents want to flourish in that life, to have a rich and happy rather than a narrow, miserable one. On this basis the slothful are clearly defective. Even if total resignation leaves them relatively content, their frame of mind is incompatible with any truly positive feelings, such as joy or love. Their emotional life must be impoverished. But beyond this, the slothful cannot be said to lead a life at all, let alone a flourishing one. They are not fully agents, in the sense that they have no projects around which to organize aspects of their lives, and hence no prospects which they might aim to realize. Any busyness they might display is without roots and without branches which reach beyond itself. Nor can they respond properly to others, for personal relationships, like everything else in their world, are not thought worth much effort, and this in turn will affect adversely the attitude of others towards them. In their withdrawal they abdicate all responsibility for themselves and their doings. One of Kierkegaard's narrators speaks of boredom as the root of all evil, ruinous to everyone,[18] and with their lack of personhood it seems quite plausible to suggest that the slothful are in the grip of the deadliest of the vices.

I spoke of the deadliness of the vices as consisting in the harm done to the self. The frame of mind of the slothful determines their view of themselves as well as that of the world. The latter is reflected in the former. Finding nothing to do in the world, they are bored with themselves. Boredom is reflexive. As in the emotional state of boredom it was the book or the conversation that was seen by the person concerned as the obstacle to her doing something with the time on hand, it is now herself in the state of inertness which is that obstacle. But of course she cannot remove herself from herself as she could remove herself from the book, nor can she comfort herself with the thought that there will shortly be an end to the boredom, for she is tied to herself as she is not tied to the conversation. The self is not the 'object' of her state in the way the book or conversation was that object.

Sloth is a paralysing vice. The slothful carry the burden of a useless self. Awareness of this condition explains occurrent moods of indolence, hopelessness, and despair. If, like Oblomov, they manage nonetheless to achieve a relatively contented state of mind then this is because they have found some mental busyness and are given to idle daydreams which may, at least for periods of time, conceal their burden from themselves. But periods of relative contentment cannot disguise sloth as an obstacle to leading any sort of life at all, and so an obstacle to functioning as an agent. In this consists its harm.

---

[18] *Either/Or*, i. 281. Also Schopenhauer, *Parerga and Paralipomena*, ii., *Psychological Remarks*, para. 358 n.: 'boredom is the source of the gravest evils'.

3 ENVY AND COVETOUSNESS

I

THE wholly slothful are unique among the vicious here selected in that they abdicate agency altogether. The 'deadliness' of their condition may be taken quite literally: they kill that which makes a person a person, they cannot be said to lead a life at all. Their lack of engagement is so thorough that it covers practical reasoning itself. They may think that they engage in such an exercise, but on those occasions when they do consider any alternative to non-action they do so only superficially and self-deceptively. In this they differ from the possessors of other vices. The latter do have aims they wish to pursue, and they accept certain types of reasons as reasons for action. The reasons' acceptability, however, depends on the respective agent's mode of perceiving the world, and this in each case provides a framework which is so defective that their practical reasoning will be self-defeating.

Envy and covetousness seem more closely related to each other than is either to the vice of sloth. Indeed, envy may conceivably be seen as one specific type of covetousness. Traditionally, covetousness, the sin of *avaritia*, was thought of quite generally as the inordinate love of wealth and the power that wealth gives (e.g. Aquinas, *Summa Theologiae* (*ST*) 2a2ae q. 118 art. 2). Such love was said to take different forms: it may manifest itself in miserly hoarding, in lavish spending, or in the persistent acquisition of wealth by whatever means. This suggests that there are three paradigm cases of covetousness, personified in the miserly avaricious, the spendthrift, and the greedy, having in common an 'unreasonable' attitude towards money or material possessions in general, but distinguishable from each other by specific features of the respective attitudes involved. I shall, in this chapter, concentrate mainly on the miserly avaricious. 'Avarice' indicates a more specific vice than does 'greed', which may be applied to lust and gluttony as well as to different forms of covetousness and envy. A spendthrift, for instance, may recklessly spend money in her greed for pleasure or luxury. Greed therefore seems to be a feature shared by a number of vices rather than to be itself a particular vice, deserving a category on its own. Nor shall I say much about the spendthrift. She may be seen to resemble the slothful in some respects, and for this reason not merit detailed discussion. At least in certain cases the persistent spendthrift (though regarded with tolerance by both Aristotle and Kant) suffers the same type of harm: the spendthrift spends wastefully, wholly without thought. She acts on every whim. The potential form of viciousness of this attitude hinges on the agent's reasons for acting in this fashion. It may be that in her view there is nothing important enough to warrant effort and prudential thought. If so, she closely resembles that slothful person whose dissatisfactions express themselves in restlessness. Or it may be that although she does see value in certain courses of actions rather than in others, she nevertheless fails to make the effort necessary to put the thought into practice. This, too, would be a form of sloth. It is a state of affairs which may force her to ward off awareness of it by acting quite without thought, a form of busyness, perhaps, and if so not conducive to the leading of a life she deems worthwhile.[1]

This leaves the miser. The miserly avaricious have to be distinguished from both the thrifty and the merely mean. None of these likes to spend money, whether on others or on herself, but for different reasons. The thrifty are concerned with the relative requirements of present and future. Wanting to use the means at their disposal in the best way possible they are prepared to forgo some benefit today in order to enjoy a, in their view greater, benefit tomorrow. In being careful with (e.g.) money today they have a specific aim relating to their or perhaps their children's future lives. They are therefore prepared to take some risk, for we cannot know what the

---

[1] Perhaps the spendthrift aims at pleasure. In that case she would in some respects share the defects of the lustful and gluttonous, to be discussed later.

future holds. The future demand envisaged by the thrifty may not materialize, and so they run the risk of uselessly forgoing some comfort or luxury. A person's circumstances may of course be such that her thrift is perfectly justified; it may be an exercise in admirable prudence. But if the thrifty take away more from the present than they should, that is, forgo what they need today and have no good reason for thinking that thereby they will be able to meet a greater need tomorrow, they move from thrift towards meanness.

The mean essentially dislike spending; this is what defines them. Meanness may grow out of the habit of thrift, or it may be due to a conviction that it is somehow sinful to spend money, so that the people concerned experience some barrier of pain or guilt. In these cases the mean are not necessarily miserly. While all misers are mean, not all the mean are miserly, for the case of the latter is more complex. Their attitude towards money or other goods is not merely negative. In contrast to the justifiably thrifty the miser, in not spending today, *appears* to think wholly in terms of future demands and hence to be prepared to take great risks. She would then be at fault merely because her risk-taking is excessive rather than rationally calculated. However, the miser does not save for the future; she does not want to spend at all, either now or later, she wants to keep her money or goods. This suggests that far from being prepared to take great risks she wants to take no risks at all. Unlike the thrifty she does not see her money as a means towards some specific end, but rather attaches value to the storing of it. It is the possession itself that is of importance to her. Such an attitude requires explanation.

Kant, in his lecture called 'The Attachment of the Mind to Wealth (Greed and Avarice)',[2] speaks of the miserly as those who love their money itself, rather than that which it enables them to acquire. They want to hoard and consequently are mean in wishing to spend as little of it as possible. In doing so they deprive themselves as well as others of much that it is in their power to acquire and enjoy. The miser, then, misguidedly thinks of the possession of money as an end in itself, whereas of course the whole point of money is

---

[2] *Lectures on Ethics.* See also his *Metaphysical First Principles of the Doctrine of Virtue,* i. *Doctrine of the Elements of Ethics,* pt. I, book 1, ch. 2, para. 10, tr. Mary Gregor (Cambridge: Cambridge University Press, 1993).

its purchasing power, enabling its possessor to use it in acquiring whatever is needed, or gives comfort or pleasure. But the miser, apparently, derives comfort and pleasure from the store of his wealth itself. This seems a paradoxical state of affairs, for in holding on to what he has got he rather seems to forgo what comfort and pleasure are at his disposal.

Kant suggests an ingenious solution to this problem. The miser, he thinks, concentrates on the pleasure of knowing that he has the power to acquire certain pleasures. The mere possession of the power to gratify one's desires is pleasant, and the miser feeds himself on the thought of the pleasures which he knows are within his reach. In this way, Kant says, 'the very possession of wealth enables him both to enjoy and to forego all pleasures'.

Kant has a point. It is true that the awareness of having the power to satisfy a desire is a pleasant one. But it is surely only one pleasure among others. There is no reason to think that such awareness is perpetually more pleasant than is at least the occasional fulfilment of another desire, and so the account offered is not a full explanation of why the miser should rest content with possibilities. To fill this gap Kant equips him with a piece of practical reasoning: the miser envisages a situation where he has spent the money and enjoyed whatever it has purchased. But such enjoyments are short-lived. So that pleasure is soon gone, gone also is the money that bought it, and with it the possibility of using it on some other pleasure. So he is really worse off than he would have been if he had not spent the money in the first place. The moral is that he had better hang on to what he has got for the envisaged future state of affairs is less attractive than are his present circumstances.

This piece of reasoning, Kant suggests, involves a fallacy. 'Avarice arises from a process of misguided logic', he says. The fallacy arises in this way: given that I have a certain amount of money I am free to spend it as I please. But once I have spent it this freedom disappears, for other objects of desire are no longer within my reach. Thoughts of this kind give rise to an illusion which takes hold of the miser: instead of thinking of his wealth *disjunctively*, as serviceable for this purpose or that, he thinks of it *conjunctively*, and imagines that it can buy whatever he wants. So as long as his money is still in his possession he can cling to the thought that all the pleasures he could possibly want are at his disposal. It must therefore be better to keep the money rather than spend it, and so money itself becomes the object of the greatest pleasure. This second move in Kant's argument is hardly convincing. This is so partly because the pleasures the miser is said to envisage are curiously restricted. Kant appears to be thinking of either pleasures of the ephemeral kind, like a good dinner or a bottle of wine, the enjoyment of which would indeed be short-lived. Or, perhaps more likely, he has in mind the swiftly passing type of pleasure which consists merely in a desire being satisfied, irrespective of whether its object in fact gratifies. But it is not clear why the miser should not envisage a more constant source of pleasure (a beautiful picture, a comfortable home) which might weigh more heavily in the scales. More importantly, however, the suggestion that avarice rests on a piece of fallacious logic is wholly implausible. A mistake in logic cannot possibly explain the impact the miser's illusion has on him. It governs his whole life. If he does engage in the sort of fallacious reasoning described then it is more likely prompted by the miserly state of mind and is not that which brings it about.

Nevertheless, Kant's initial remarks point in the right direction. It is true, I think, that it is possession of a power or capacity the miser treasures, and it is true that this attachment rests on a delusion. But what sort of power is it he imagines he has acquired and which is of such importance to him that he feels he has to cling to it? Typically at least, he does not seem to be considering the range of pleasures which are possibilities at his disposal while he keeps his hoard; rather, his desires and their satisfaction seem concentrated wholly on the store itself:

Gradually the guineas, the crowns, and the half-crowns, grew to a heap, and Marner drew less and less for his own wants, trying to solve the problem of keeping himself strong enough to work sixteen hours a day on as small an outlay as possible . . . Marner wanted the heaps of ten to grow into a square, and then into a larger square; and every added guinea, while it was itself a satisfaction, bred a new desire . . . the money not only grew, but it remained with him . . . He handled them (the coins), he counted them, till their form and colour were like the satisfaction of a thirst to him.   (George Eliot, *Silas Marner*, ch. 2).

Marner, like any miser, sees his possession of the money as a most desirable good. Such a good can hardly consist in the actual properties of the actual coins. If the handling of golden guineas was itself a pleasure then it can have been only an incidental one, not perhaps as great for those who have to be content with cheaper metal or with paper, and absent altogether if the wealth is accumulated in a bank account. They miss out on that extra pleasure of seeing concrete proof of their power. But that which makes the hoard of money of such overwhelming importance to its owner must be in what it is taken to represent, which in turn is taken to confer certain capacities on its possessor.

Most obviously, money may be taken to represent status, power, security, or pleasure, and the possession of money, therefore, confers the capacity on its owner to impress with status, to exercise power, to feel secure, or to enjoy a range of pleasures. But it confers no more than the capacity, the realization of which will require some use of it. This is what the miser does not appear to see. He clings to the possession and guards it against all possible incursion. He wants to keep it safe, he wants to be secure in the knowledge that it is his. The structure of the misers' attitude is therefore complex: they see, rightly, that the possession of money represents a range of desirable goods and hence puts them in a favourable position. But they also think, misguidedly, that they can secure this position for themselves, and that security can be achieved by keeping hold of their possession, i.e. by never using the capacity they have acquired. If what they see money as representing is power, then they want to feel secure in their possession of power; if it is security, then they want their security assured. And in some cases, perhaps, they wish, as Kant suggests, to secure the possibility of enjoying innumerable pleasures.

Kant made the mistake of taking one possible case, the desire to ensure the possibility of fulfilling any want one might have, as being the crux of the matter. But basically the desire is for security of possession, and the potential availability of pleasures only one specific and perhaps not very likely instance of what it is the miser wishes to be certain of. Even more unsatisfactory is the route by means of which the miser is supposed to have reached his position. The explanation in terms of a piece of fallacious reasoning not only ascribes to such reasoning an influence over a person's life which it is unlikely to possess, it also suggests that the agent's view of what to aim at is consciously achieved, by reflecting on the alternatives open to him. This, too, is hardly likely. The miser does not think of himself as pointlessly storing a capacity without the intention of exercising it. On the contrary, he will be inclined to see himself as sagaciously taking precautions against a rainy day. But his characteristic desires and actions do not bear this out. They rather suggest that it is apprehension or fear which motivates him and that in the store he clings to he sees a guarantee that he is secure in occupying whatever the position he imagines it bestows upon him. Spending it, using the capacity, would be to take the risk of losing that position. His misperceptions, then, are symptomatic of some urgent need, and not the result of misguided calculations.

Unlike the thrifty the miser means to take no risk whatever. He is misguided not merely in setting such store by a mere capacity; he is wholly deluded in thinking that the type of security and reassurance he is after is available at all. His clinging to his store is a consequence of this delusion, for he regards his hoard as the guarantee that his position is his forever. But, circumstances of human life being what they are, there cannot be such a guarantee. There is no time at which the miser can rest content, having achieved his aim. On the contrary, he will always have to be on his guard against possible threats and incursions, constantly and obsessively concerned with keeping his hoard intact. Since his desire for guaranteed security of position is always frustrated he must perpetually continue to seek its fulfilment. Consequently, rather than looking outward or ahead to the future he has to concentrate his thoughts on his accumulated stock. His vision will accordingly be a very narrow one.

His store, in the miser's view, is that which protects him. It is for this reason that he has to cling to it. To let go is to make himself vulnerable. But the attempt to thus protect oneself is self-defeating and irrational, and the thought that it can be achieved harmfully self-deceptive: in narrowly focusing on the aim of self-protection he prevents himself from properly assessing his circumstances and hence corrupts his belief-forming processes and capacity for sane judgement. His attitude to the world and in particular to others is not rational. In so far as his beliefs concern himself and his fantasy of a position of security they are self-deceptive. To maintain the fantasy further beliefs have to fit into the given system and so the self-deception is continually reaffirmed and becomes more deeply rooted. He cannot afford to be open to any evidence which threatens to undermine his beliefs. Nor of course can he admit his view of the world and of himself to be misguided. He has to represent the fantasy-world in which he is imprisoned as being rationally constructed, the outcome of clear thought and sound reasoning. Kant remarks (in his lecture) that misers always have an excuse for their being so intent on saving and 'generally say that they save against bad times or for their relatives'. But thinking themselves justified is part of the whole web of self-deception, both necessitated by their emotional commitment, and also feeding it.

Self-deception and irrationality of beliefs and judgement are inevitable given the nature of the miser's emotional commitment. Since he clings to something which he thinks will provide him with what he needs but which it is not capable of providing, his search for assurance must be self-defeating. Entrenched as his desires are he cannot bring himself to spell out to himself the futility of his enterprise, though his clinging to his store, and his jealous guard over it, may indicate some suppressed awareness of the situation. But since he does not think through and is not prepared to re-evaluate his position his natural response is to cling even more closely to what he has got and to guard it ever more jealously. This picture of a deeply entrenched delusion indicates the damage the miserly avaricious will suffer. There is a basic conflict in their situation, for the very desire to feel assured of their position breeds anxiety, which leads to the desire for further assurance, and so, since this cannot be had, to yet more anxiety.

The misers' situation is such that they will live in a claustrophobic world from within which the outside world will appear a hostile and threatening place. The misers we meet in literature conform to this characterization. Silas Marner, during his miserly period, is a solitary figure whose only friends are his guineas. When these are stolen from him he feels 'the withering desolation of bereavement'. His life had been filled 'with an immediate purpose which fenced him in from the wide, cheerless unknown'; now that his treasure is lost his soul is left 'like a forlorn traveler on an unknown desert' (chs. 10 and 5). His store of coins had clearly been to him a protection from an indifferent world which he had to hang on to in order not to expose his vulnerability. Dickens's Scrooge, a very different kind of man, is equally isolated, he is 'secret and self-contained, and solitary as an oyster' (*A Christmas Carol*, stave 1). His self-defence—unlike that of Marner—expresses itself aggressively, in open hostility towards others who therefore naturally shrink from him. Molière's miser, the wealthy Harpagon, not only makes his children's life a misery with his 'unnatural parsimony', he is also deeply suspicious of all who come to the house, believing them, including his own children, to have the one aim of getting hold of his treasure. He thinks that he is being constantly watched, that there are spies everywhere devouring everything he possesses and rummaging everywhere to see whether there is more that might be worth stealing (*The Miser*, Act 1). To him others are nothing but a threat and the world a wholly hostile place.

The miserly avaricious, then, defeat their own purposes. The possession of money which is supposed to be of such value to them does, on the contrary, lead to frustration. They live in a shrinking world and lose control over their lives, for they are at the mercy of their dominating desire. Aquinas speaks of their desires as being 'inordinate', and of their loving the wrong object (*ST* 2a2ae q. 118). Their desires may be taken to be 'inordinate' or 'excessive' in a number of directions: they are obsessive and self-perpetuating and dominate their lives. The wrong object which they love is in Aquinas's view not the material good as such, but themselves as the owner of such possession. More precisely, the loved object may be described as 'the self assured of its possession'. This is a self-protective love; it is misdirected because there is no such self. Consequently this first self-protective love prompts a second, namely, the self-deception needed to protect the first self-love from being seen to be misplaced. Their complex aim of self-protection confirms the miser's desires as being 'inordinate' or excessive, especially so because their being left unsatisfied demands their constant renewal. The misdirected self-love enforces inordinate desires. So the miserly avaricious become more and more cocooned in the delusion that they are hanging on to something of great value.

I have concentrated on the paradigm case of the miser where what he hoards is money itself. His case is the clearest and the most obvious one to need explanation. Yet the sin of *avaritia* was the sin of loving

excessively any kind of material possession. The difference between
the case discussed and the hoarder of other material goods is that
the latter's position may strike one as perfectly reasonable. Where,
for instance, these goods are works of art it seems quite natural
that their owner might wish to keep them because they provide a
constant source of aesthetic pleasure. Works of art are not thought of
as something to be used. Balzac's Cousin Pons, for example, derives
much pleasure from his collection of paintings and bric-a-brac, and
it is not surprising that he does not wish to part from it. Yet he
is described as 'a miser at heart' (ch. 2). And the description is not
misplaced for there are structural resemblances in his desires and
attitudes to those displayed by the paradigmatically miserly. He,
as they, guards his collection jealously; he, as they, clings to his
possession even though the money acquired by the sale of just a few
items would enable him to satisfy his desires for fine food and wine,
and would provide him with the kind of care he needs when ill. The
indications are that there is more at stake than merely the experience
of aesthetic pleasure, that he, too, sees his possessions as representing
some form of security. In his case, as well as in that of some of
the others referred to, some light is thrown on their position when
we learn more about them or their backgrounds. Cousin Pons saw
himself as unloved and unlovable; Silas Marner had been betrayed by
a friend and unjustly expelled from his community; and Scrooge had
an unhappy, embittering childhood. They all were in need of some
reassurance.

Unlike the traditional sin, the vice of avarice need not be confined
to the world of material possessions. George Eliot, having described
the state of mind of her miser Silas Marner, adds that there are other
types of misers, only instead of a heap of guineas they have 'some
erudite research, some ingenious project, or some well-knit theory'
(ch. 2). She offers no further explanation, but the here proposed
structure of the vice allows for such cases. One of Eliot's own
characters may serve as a possible example: the scholar Mr Casaubon
devotes his life to his great work on the key to all Mythologies. He
clings to this work as another type of miser clings to his guineas. But
it is clear that his massive notes will never turn into a publishable
book, and clear that Casaubon's theory would not survive the scrutiny
of a detached scholar. He cannot admit this to himself for doing so

would reveal to himself that he can no longer think of himself as a distinguished scholar engaged in most valuable research. But this is what gives meaning to his life. So, like other misers, he has to protect his treasure: he works in isolation avoiding all contact with other scholars; he is irritated by and evades searching questions; he refuses to learn German and so does not explore what is essential to his studies:

Poor Mr. Casaubon himself was lost among small closets and winding stairs, and in an agitated dimness about the Cabeiri, or in an exposure of other mythologists' ill-considered parallels, easily lost sight of any purpose which had prompted him to these labours. With his taper stuck before him he forgot the absence of windows, and in bitter manuscript remarks on other men's notions about the solar deities, he had become indifferent to the sunlight. (*Middlemarch*, ch. 20)

Poor Mr Casaubon had to become indifferent to the sunlight, for facing it would bring the insight that his work is futile and that his life's preoccupations and his conception of himself are a delusion.

II

There is, clearly, no sharp dividing line between avarice and greed. The miserly like to see their store increase, for the larger the treasure the better the protection. So they may easily slip into greed, wanting more and more, possibly at whatever cost to others. Greed in turn may be accompanied by envy: the greedy may want for themselves what they see others as having. There is thus a natural connection between these vices. There is also a structural similarity between avarice and envy. The viciously envious, like the miserly avaricious, are caught in a delusion and are forced to deceive themselves.

Envy rests on interpersonal comparison. The envious person thinks of another as being in some way better off than she is herself. Everyday expressions of envy often indicate no more than that the speaker sees merit in some possession or experience the other has and she lacks. 'I envy you your beautiful garden, having seen the Russian Ballet, going round the world . . .' may mean no more than that one can appreciate the point of what the other has and think that it might be nice to have or experience such things oneself. But this may be no more than a short-lived idle wish. Conventional expressions of envy need not indicate any particular emotional response at all and are for present purposes irrelevant. But even setting these aside and concentrating only on cases where the person seriously minds being at a comparative disadvantage, expressions of envy may still be ambiguous. Distinguishable types are not marked when we speak of envying some person because of her possession of a certain good. Given this ambiguity it is not surprising that in the relevant literature we find a divergence of views as to the classification of envy. There is general agreement that where it is a vice it is a particularly nasty one, but not everyone takes the view that envy is always a vice.

Descartes, for instance, explicitly states that he uses the word 'envy' to signify a passion which is not always vicious.[3] Envy, he thinks, is a kind of sadness mingled with hatred which proceeds from our seeing good coming to those we consider unworthy of it. If the other really is unworthy in that he makes bad use of the good, then our love of justice makes the feeling excusable, provided our hatred relates to the misuse and not to the present possessor of the good.

Rawls is in sympathy with the point that a sense of justice may make feelings of envy at any rate excusable:

> Yet sometimes the circumstances invoking envy are so compelling that given human beings as they are no one can reasonably be asked to overcome his rancorous feelings. A person's lesser position as measured by the index of objective primary goods may be so great as to wound his self-respect; and given his situation, we may sympathize with his sense of loss.[4]

So perhaps envy may be excusable or even justified. Descartes adds to considerations of justice a further condition for excusable envy along the lines of 'hate the sin but not the sinner'. This stipulation is of interest not so much for the pious sentiment it expresses but

---

[3] René Descartes, *Passions of the Soul*, art. 182.

[4] John Rawls, *A Theory of Justice* (Oxford: Oxford University Press, 1973), pt. 3, ch. 9, sect. 81.

because it points to a distinction between two types of envy which will help to clarify the question of when envy is and when it may not be vicious.

By analogy with the distinction between the sin and the sinner, we should distinguish between the possessor of the good on the one hand, and the good possessed on the other. Consequently there are two possible targets on which the thoughts and feelings of the envious person may focus, and based on this distinction we can characterize two types of envy, which I shall label respectively 'object-' and 'state-envy'. In cases of object-envy the envy is of the good the other has; its possessor plays a relatively minor role as being merely the occasion for the envious person's realization of her deficiencies. Perception of the other's possession of the good turns her attention to irritating or even humiliating thoughts about her lack of it, but the possessor of the desired good plays no prominent role in her consciousness. In state-envy, on the other hand, the envy is of the-other-having-that-good. Here the other is seen as not merely that which happens to prompt her disagreeable view of herself, but is thought of as somehow crucially involved in her finding herself in an inferior position. Object-envy may of course merge into state-envy, particularly if the occasion for it is frequent and proximate.

It is object-envy that is not vicious in the sense here understood. For it may not merely not drastically harm the agent, it may even be beneficial to her. She may admire those who possess the good and strive to improve her own position in the relevant respect. So it may motivate her to lead a richer and more satisfactory life, and, if successful, will spare her unfavourable comparisons in the future. This does not mean, however, that such envy is necessarily a good thing. Whether it is or not will depend largely on whether what she admires is in fact admirable, whether there is some reasoned justification for her view. Equally, object-envy may harm the agent in that realization of her inferiority, far from inspiring her to try and better herself, may on the contrary depress her with the thought that she is doomed to a lowly station. Such an attitude may leave her in the grip of a vice, but if so, it would be the vice of sloth, or perhaps of a form of anger, rather than that of envy.

There is a well-known way of avoiding such harm: the envious may belittle the relevant goods and persuade themselves that they are not worth having. They get involved in the 'sour grapes syndrome'.[5] A clear example of precisely this attitude is provided by Proust. In *Swann's Way* Marcel remarks of his great-aunt: 'Whenever she saw in others an advantage, however trivial, which she herself lacked, she would persuade herself that it was no advantage at all, but a drawback, and would pity so as not to envy them' (*À la recherche du temps perdu*, i. ch. 1). Such evasive moves, if she manages to convince herself, are presumably helpful in saving her from feelings of inferiority. They are also corruptive to a greater or lesser degree in that they can only confuse the agent's evaluations. But if it is only object-envy she is suppressing then she will not be exposed to the destructive harm brought about by vicious envy.

Object-envy is not usually what we have in mind when we think of a person as envious, particularly not where its effect consists in motivating the agent to try for greater achievement. And even where its impact is negative, where the good in question is (self-deceptively) belittled, it may not do much harm, or, where it does, may be the manifestation of some vice (e.g. pride) other than envy itself. It is in any case not the worst form of envy, and by some would not be picked out as envy at all. For it lacks what is often thought to be a crucial feature: a degree of hostility directed against those seen as the possessor of the desirable good. To accommodate this feature we have to turn to state-envy.

The focus of state-envy is the others' 'state' of occupying a comparatively advantageous position; it is their possession of the good rather than the good itself. The envious person wants to see this advantage removed. Again there are alternatives: she may do so by improving her own position in relation to that of the other. This I shall label 'emulative envy'. Or she may try and spoil the other's advantage.

---

[5] Thomas Reid, *Essays on the Active Powers of the Human Mind*, Essay III, 'Of Malevolent Affection', uses the 'sour grapes' case to distinguish 'pure envy' from 'fair and honest emulation', which consists in the effort to do better than one's rival. But since he does not distinguish between object- and state-envy different strands remain entangled. Emulation does not seem to me to be always 'fair and honest', for reasons to be explained later. Moreover, the sour grapes in his account are expressed not merely in belittling the relevant good, but also by looking with an evil eye on his competitor, and the attempt to throw a stumbling block in his way. But this is not a feature of those given to merely object-envy.

This is destructive state-envy. Emulative envy may be thought to be a good thing, for it, like the positive form of object-envy (called 'admiring envy' for ease of distinction), will encourage the agent to try for better things. This seems to be the view of e.g. Rawls when he says that emulative envy 'leads us to try to achieve what others have. The sight of their greater good moves us to strive in socially beneficial ways for similar things for ourselves' (*A Theory of Justice*, p. 533). This view seems over-optimistic. The problem is not just that the striving need not be socially beneficial, as it is assumed to be in Rawls's setting. The envied person may, for all we know, be the chief of a group of gangsters. More importantly, 'emulation' here has the implication, lacking in the case of admiring envy, of rivalry and competition. The other is seen as a rival whose success is somehow linked with one's own failure. He is therefore likely to be regarded as a thorn in one's flesh, attracting feelings of resentment. Resentment in itself is a self-corruptive emotion (see Ch. 5.), and the temptation to harm the other is likely to be quite strong. The danger of sliding into destructive envy is greater here than it was in cases of admiring envy, and so perhaps it is not a state to encourage.

It is, however, not emulative but destructive envy which is the candidate for the deadly vice. What is to be destroyed, if only by belittling it, is not the good in question, but is the position of the possessor of that good. So here we have a form of the sour grapes syndrome which is related to that to be found in negative object-envy as emulative envy was related to admiring envy. It is exemplified by Iago's attitude towards Cassio, recently appointed by Othello as his lieutenant. Iago says of him:

> . . . mere prattle, without practice
> Is all his soldiership. But he, Sir, had the election;
> And I, of whom his eyes had seen the proof
> At Rhodes, at Cyprus . . .
> And I, God bless the mark! his Moorship's ancient. (*Othello* I. i. 26 ff.)

Iago here aims at (verbally) destroying Cassio-the-suitable-occupier-of-a-military-position, which Iago thought was due to him. In his view, Cassio has taken something which was his by right, and so Cassio—together with Othello—is causally responsible for Iago's comparative disadvantage. It is because Cassio occupies the superior position that Iago cannot have it.

From one point of view the envy expressed by Iago may be seen as 'primitive'. It is primitive in that the other is seen as (at least partially) causally responsible for his own disadvantaged state. Small children are capable of feeling envy of this type, and so, at any rate according to Melanie Klein, are very young infants. According to her theory in *Envy and Gratitude* the infant, realizing that the source of food and comfort is outside herself, assumes that when she is deprived of these goods they are enjoyed by the breast itself, and so has the impulse to destroy it. Typically in all cases of primitive envy the other is seen as keeping for herself that which the child thinks should be his. Feelings of hostility are a natural consequence of this perception: the destruction of the other as the source of his own discomfort and frustration is a form of retaliation and has a point, therefore, even if it does not result in his gaining possession of that good. In so far as Iago's envy has these features it is of the primitive type.

On the other hand, envying a person their status is rather different from envying them their toys. Consequently, Iago's envy will also have characteristics which make his envy 'sophisticated'. Sophistic-ated envy differs from the primitive kind in that it can be felt only by those who have self-consciousness, who have an image of themselves and of their standing in the world. This is one respect in which this type of envy is 'sophisticated'. It is also sophisticated in that, in contrast to primitive envy, the other is here not seen as having deprived her of the desirable good itself, as being the direct cause of her being without it. It is clear that not all cases of envy can be of the primitive kind, where the other is seen in exactly these terms. The ugly sisters may envy Cinderella her beauty, but it would be inane of them to think that they lack beauty *because* she has it. Irrational though envy may well be, it would be wholly implausible to explain all cases where what is envied is another's possession of a personal quality such as beauty, or courage, or power, in terms of the person's irrational belief in a direct causal connection between his possession of it and her own lack. The role of the other as a threatening figure has here to be accounted for differently.

In cases of sophisticated envy the other's possession of some good or occupation of a certain position is seen as the source not primarily of our not having them, but of our being seen to lack them. Cinderella's beauty brings it home to the world and to the ugly sisters themselves that they are not beautiful; Cassio's appointment impresses on the world and on Iago himself that he is not thought to have the qualities which would make him a good lieutenant. The circumstances of the other are a threat because they spoil the view one wants others and particularly oneself to be able to take of one's own position. Either way they are a threat to one's self-esteem.

Primitive and sophisticated envy may of course coincide, as they do in Iago's case. The envious person may see the other as depriving her of the actual good which she wants for herself and thereby as also destroying the image she wishes to impress on both herself and others. On the other hand, sophisticated envy may be felt by a person who does not want precisely the position occupied by the other, or does not want to possess herself the sorts of qualities the other has. Iago might be envious of Cassio even if he thinks the position of lieutenant too troublesome for comfort and does not really wish to occupy it. It is true that if envious feelings are not to remain quite inexplicable the good in question has to be seen as being in some way desirable, but this need not imply that it is possession of the good itself that is desired. It may be seen as being seen to be desirable by others, by members of the society where one wishes to be well thought of. Being seen to possess that good would thus enhance one's status. Conversely, being plainly seen to lack it would lower one's status in the eyes of others and diminish their esteem. It is the other who enjoys their admiration, and it is the view of the other seen as esteem-worthy which is such poison. Loss of self-esteem is the inevitable consequence, either because the agent agrees that lack of the good is demeaning, or because she sets great store by the view (some) others take of her. If she thought little of the value of having the good, and little of what others think of her, she would not have felt envy in the first place. In sophisticated envy the perceived threat of the other's possession of the good is that the comparison will lead to recognition of lack or loss of status and esteem.

Sophisticated envy, then, allows for the possibility that the envious person values neither the relevant good itself nor possession of that good. The worth of what the other has may be merely, in her view, in it being the means towards a desirable end: a certain status and the approval, admiration, and esteem that brings with it. But such a status is not hers, and so the next best thing is to try and bring it about that others and she herself should not be constantly reminded of this humiliating state of affairs. The other is held responsible not, or not necessarily, for her own lack of certain qualities or positions, but for being a reminder of that discrepancy, and hence for depriving her of the possibility of ignoring that state of affairs, or of pretending that it is different. The destruction of the other as the possessor of the good is therefore a natural aim.

The central presence of other-directed destructive thoughts and desires may itself be sufficient to explain why envy is deemed to be a particularly nasty vice. Especially in those cases where the envious person does not particularly care to possess the good itself such hostility appears to be pure spite, a grudgingness for its own sake. Envy is said to spoil the good it covets, and certainly, to destroy at least in wishful thought the desired good in another's possession is one way of spoiling his advantage. As Nozick says, the envious person prefers not having the good provided the other does not have it, to him having it while she lacks it.[6] The implication is that there is something paradoxical about this vice: if the child breaks the other's toy which she wants for herself then she has hardly improved her own situation. Spoiling the coveted good means that the envious person can never have what she wants, that she will necessarily be frustrated. In primitive envy the only advantage which could conceivably be said to accrue to her was seen to be the satisfaction of her desires for revenge. More is at stake in cases of sophisticated envy.

In (destructive) sophisticated envy the desired good in question is an esteem-worthy self. This is what the envious person perceives the other as having and herself as lacking. So she feels frustrated and caught in her inferior position. She has to ward off the recognition of her inferiority, and ward off consequent feelings of shame and humiliation. Otherwise her self-esteem would be further undermined. So she escapes from the threat by attacking that which she sees as responsible for her plight. This move is partially analogous to the spoiling of the other's toy, on the principle that what I cannot

---

[6] Robert Nozick, *Anarchy, State and Utopia* (Oxford: Basil Blackwell, 1974).

have another shall not have, either. But here there are further repercussions. The envious person desires an esteem-worthy self. She also desires the disappearance of those whose contrasting position impresses this need on her and forces her to face what she sees as her own lowly standing. Rather than have her thoughts so directed she turns away from herself and aggressively towards the other. From one point of view this is a not unreasonable reaction, for it allows her to cling to a relatively peaceful state of mind. How else is she to preserve it? She cannot, after all, magically all at once improve her own position.[7]

On the other hand, such a destructive move cannot possibly help her to achieve her aim of being esteem-worthy. On the contrary, in attempting to disguise the deficiency she prevents herself from taking any positive steps in the right direction. In blaming the other for bringing about her plight she protects herself from an awareness which would add to her discomfort. Her state is then truly paradoxical: her desire to attain a certain good is frustrated by the desire to remove any reminder that she still lacks that good.

Destructive sophisticated envy is a self-protective emotion or attitude. But what is it that it protects? It cannot be an esteem-worthy self, for this is what the agent thinks she lacks by comparison with the other. So what she protects is a self she herself does not think much of; if she did she would not so keenly desire an esteem-worthy self in the first place. She protects the, in her own view, defective self by further attempting to protect the *appearance* of an esteem-worthy self which she and others can, deceptively, be expected to respect. Other-directed destructive thoughts, desires, or actions serve the end of diverting her attention from what she thinks of as defects in herself, and hence saves her from having to suffer self-directed hostility. This is the rationale of envy. But in seeking self-protection she gets herself involved in a web of frustrations and contradictions, for the desired

---

[7] Max Scheler, *Ressentiment*, tr. W. W. Holdheim (New York: Schocken, 1972), ch. 1, thinks that the owner of the coveted good is always *falsely* considered to be the cause of the deprivation. But this depends on what the agent is thought to be deprived of. If it is her (temporarily) tranquil state of mind then the other is correctly seen as the cause of the deprivation. But Scheler is right in emphasizing the feeling of impotence involved in envy of this type.

aim cannot be achieved but is undermined by other-directed hostile thoughts and desires. The self, in her own suppressed view, remains defective. The coveted good, the esteem-worthy self, is indeed spoilt in this type of envy.

This state of affairs cannot be a happy one for the person concerned. Her self-deception has to be maintained and indeed nursed carefully, for, given the likelihood or anyway possibility of being reminded of the other's status, she has repeatedly to prevent herself from realizing the futility of her ways. Such a degree of self-deception must leave her insecure, always on the look-out for further threatened revelations. It will also confuse both her aims and her evaluations. Concerned as she is with self-esteem she has yet left herself no clear view as to how it ought to be based and how it could be fostered.

It is clearly a hopeless undertaking to substitute destruction of the other's good for the obtaining of that good for oneself. That was the position of the viciously envious. But even destructive sophisticated envy may conceivably, in very specific circumstances, be not unreasonable from the agent's point of view, at least theoretically. It may also be understandable and excusable. These two cases have to be kept apart. For this type of envy not to be unreasonable it has to be the case that the esteem-worthiness of the other is, on good grounds, believed to attach to his position and only his position, so that to gain that is also to gain the esteem-worthy self. The grounds for this belief have to be good to preclude the case where the envious person misreads the situation precisely because she is in the grip of envy. The conditions for not unreasonable envy are then very specific and it is hardly conceivable that, life being what it is, they will ever be found to be fulfilled. First, the case of envy has to be one like Iago's where primitive and sophisticated envy coincide: the desire for the good, the military position, coincides with the desire for esteem. Secondly, the setting, one has to assume, is of the type of a military society where honour and esteem hinge exclusively on one's position in the hierarchy. Here the wished-for destruction of the owner-of-the-good is not by means of spoiling the good; the aim is rather to spoil the relation between owner and good by ruining the owner, by demoting, shaming, or killing him. This would leave open the possibility that a Iago may occupy the coveted position and so fulfil his desire. But it is only a possibility in given circumstances, for normally there is no guarantee that the removal of the envied other means that the position is automatically his. Othello may not want Iago to be his lieutenant under any circumstances. And normally, of course, the case is not so simple. Cassio's status is after all only one causal factor among others accounting for Iago's attitude. Not unreasonable vicious envy, then, remains at best a theoretical possibility.

On this level envy is not unreasonable from the agent's point of view because the desires involved are not necessarily conflicting and frustrating. It is consequently not vicious in the sense of not being necessarily self-corruptive. But this is not to say that envy of this kind may not, in its destructiveness, be unreasonable from other points of view. Nor need it be understandable and excusable. For this to be plausible further conditions have to be fulfilled. Descartes stipulates that the other is really unworthy of the good and misuses it. Rawls offers a more precise characterization when he gives such envy the context of an extremely unjust society where the deprivation of the least favoured is such as to wound their self-respect. So for envy to be understandable and excusable at least this further condition has to be added: the other's position must be (reasonably) believed to interfere harmfully and unjustly with the welfare of the envious person. For the Iago-type person to fulfil this condition he must also have the well-grounded view that he has all the right qualities for a high military position while his rival Cassio lacks them, so that the latter's appointment was unjust and his own career unfairly ruined. This type of envy is understandable and excusable because the remedy for the situation is primarily to be looked for in an alteration of the social and administrative conditions assumed, rather than in the agent himself. But even in this case envy can hardly be said to be justified, partly because any action taken as a consequence may be socially disastrous, and, in the present context more relevantly, because the feelings of other-directed resentment involved in envy always adversely affect those who nourish them (Ch. 5).

In these cases of possibly non-vicious envy it was crucial that the-owner-of-the-good and the good itself could be taken apart, so that destruction of the relationship did not harm the good. Where

conversely the two wholly coincide we have possibly the worst case
of envy. It is what Scheler calls 'existential envy'.[8] Here the mere
fact of the other's existence is resented and unforgivable, and his
destruction an ever more urgently desired aim. An example might be
Balzac's Cousin Bette whose envy of her cousin Madame Hulot and
her family is so all-absorbing that her whole life is organized around
her desire for revenge. She watches members of the family 'like a
spider in the centre of her web' and rejoices at any misfortune that
befalls them: 'She is paying for her days of good fortune now, and
that suits me ... It's her turn to bite the dust'.[9]

In all its forms, vicious envy spoils the good it covets. In this, as
in other respects, the structural features of this vice resemble those
of avarice. As in the case of avarice the desired good is not the
superficially obvious one, namely, others' and one's own possessions
respectively. The object of their desire is, in each case, a more
fundamental one, namely the self under a specific description. The
avaricious want that self to be secure, the envious want it to be
esteemed. In each case their desire for such a self must be frustrated.
In nonetheless pursuing their aim, they show themselves to be both
confused in their evaluations and also self-deceived. The desire to
cling to one's own and the desire to spoil what the other has make
it impossible for them to achieve their aim. The desires constitutive
of each vice are in conflict, but awareness of this state would be too
painful to face. In each case, therefore, they have to protect themselves
by weaving a web of self-deception which will only further entangle
them in their confusions and prevent them from finding a route of
escape.

---

[8] 'The most powerful envy is also the most terrible. Therefore *existential envy*,
which is directed against the other person's very *nature*, is the strongest source of
ressentiment.' Ibid. 52, italics in the text.

[9] Honoré de Balzac, *Cousin Bette* (Hasmondsworth: Penguin, 1965), 178 and 171.

4 SELF AND SELF-CONSCIOUSNESS

THE envious and the miserly avaricious were harmfully self-deceived. Both were self-protective, the miser of a self assured of its security, the envious of the appearance of an esteem-worthy one to veil its defects from others and particularly from herself. In both cases their desires were self-defeating. To support the claim that possession of the vices selected is self-corruptive more needs to be said about the nature of that self.

To speak of the self is to concentrate wholly on psychological aspects of the individual. In contrast to the concept of the person, it makes no reference to physical characteristics or spatial position. Nor is it a normative concept, as that of the person is usually taken to be. Intuitively, the self is thought of as a unity which can be experienced only from inside. We think of ourselves as remaining the same continuing entity through even quite dramatic changes. Whatever the criteria of identity for 'the same self' may be—if indeed there are any—they do not obviously coincide with those for personal identity. So, for instance, St Paul will have thought of himself as the same self before and after his sudden conversion to Christianity on the way to Damascus, but may well have regarded himself as a different person, no longer Saul, but Paul.[1] It is this intuitive, pre-theoretical notion of the self which is employed in the following discussion. Notoriously, the difficulties raised by the metaphysical implications of this notion have been enormous. For the self seems to emerge as a mysterious entity which unifies experience and so cannot itself be experienced.

---

[1] Colin McGinn discusses relevant puzzle cases in *The Character of Mind* (Oxford: Oxford University Press, 1982), ch. 6, where he sets out different theories of the self and their shortcomings.

The only alternatives seem to be to deny such an entity altogether, or to give it a very special and not altogether intelligible status. The self is then either no more than Hume's 'bundle of perceptions' or is a Kantian 'noumenal self'. It is true, of course, that the self cannot be experienced as one complete thing, as an entity to be grasped as a whole. But this is not surprising, for the self is no one given whole that can be met with in either sense—experience or some form of intuition. It does not follow that there are no relevant experiences at all. Experiences are experienced as one's own. For this to be possible the agent in question must be capable of self-consciousness.

The state of the miserly and of the envious implies self-consciousness, implies, that is, that the person concerned perceives certain experiences as her own and so can distinguish between herself and them, and can see herself as persisting through various experiences. They are all her experiences. The self cannot be thought of as merely a bundle of perceptions, where this is understood as a heap of data held together by only temporal relations. If this were all there was to it we could make no sense whatever of our lives. This is so because the data supposedly making up the 'bundle' are curiously neutral, indifferent as to whose experiences they are. But as experiences contributing to the self they have to be felt from inside as being one's own, and so to be connected because one's own. But for this to be possible the connection between them cannot be merely that of temporal relation but must be of a more substantial kind. The substantial connection consists in their being interpreted and assessed, seen as reasons for responses and actions, as the grounds for making decisions and forming intentions. So a person will also think of herself as having a certain amount of control, as being an agent and not a mere recipient of data. Experiences are the basis of the picture she has of herself, but they are also dependent on that picture: they are shaped, and their shape is influenced by that of earlier experiences which themselves influence that of experiences to come. It is this shape which gives coherence and continuity to the self. The particular shape imposed on experiences will be consequent (among other things) on the kinds of aims and preferences she forms, on her desires and evaluations, on how she sees herself as conducting her life. It will be her identity. The view she takes of herself is therefore constitutive of her individual self; it (partially) creates it.

This feature of self-creation may be implied by Hume's view that the self is a 'fiction', and is explicitly set out in more recent accounts of the self in terms of 'narrative' or 'inner story'.[2] The self as here understood is that which gives a person her identity as she herself sees it, and that means that she has sufficient complexity to be able to form intentions, to evaluate and select. The self is clearly no one identifiable object of consciousness. On the contrary, self-consciousness is itself constitutive of the self, and constituent of the self are consequently evaluations and decisions about what it is worthwhile to do and what to avoid, about the sort of life one wants to lead, the kind of person one wants to be. The interdependence of the elements of the shape of experiences means that they will be 'edited', that some experiences will be seen as important and others as negligible according to how they fit into already existing frameworks of beliefs and inclinations. Consequently there will always be experience-material which the agent has ignored but which may nonetheless exercise an influence over her reactions and decisions. If so, reference to such aspects of experiences may well be explanatory of what she thinks and does. On the other hand, they will not provide her with reasons for thinking or acting, they will not be her reasons for thinking this or doing that. As well as suppressing some, the agent may also allow an unreasonably exaggerated importance and pervading influence to other experiences. Both, suppression and exaggeration, give rise to the possibility of misguided self-creation, and so may create a possible niche for the notion of a 'false self'.

Self-consciousness may range over consciousness-of-experiences-had-by-oneself to consciousness-of-oneself-as-the-owner-of-these-experiences. That is, the 'object', or focus, of self-consciousness may be primarily the world as it strikes the person concerned, so that her evaluations of herself and of the sort of life she wants to lead will be implicit in what she thinks about the world and how she acts in it. Her self-consciousness will be explicit if her

---

[2] David Hume, *A Treatise of Human Nature*, bk. 1, pt. 4, sect. 6. For recent accounts see e.g. A. MacIntyre, *After Virtue* (London: Duckworth, 1981), esp. ch. 15; J. Glover, *I: The Philosophy and Psychology of Personal Identity* (Harmondsworth: Penguin, 1988), p. I; C. Taylor, *Sources of the Self* (Cambridge: Cambridge University Press, 1989), ch. 7.

concentration and concern are primarily on herself and on her role in the world. Wholly explicit self-consciousness is the extreme at one end of the range, wholly implicit the extreme at the other; at one end of the scale the person sees the world wholly in terms of her own position in it, all her thoughts, feelings, and desires concentrate only on that. At this extreme her own self is the centre of that agent's universe, and self-centredness is her essence. At the other extreme the agent gives no specific thought at all to her own position. Normally, no doubt, self-consciousness is not of either of these extreme types, which represent total self-preoccupation and total self-oblivion respectively. Normally self-consciousness varies between the explicit and the implicit—and the one may not always be distinguishable from the other.

Agents whose basic point of view is wholly that of explicit self-consciousness will locate all their experiences within that framework. Their experiences of the world will always be experiences of themselves in the world, whether or not they themselves articulate their thoughts in these terms. All the desires of the wholly self-centred will be what Bernard Williams has called 'I-desires': they will be of the form 'I want that I . . .', where the proposition is completed by the description of some state of affairs which the agent sees as desirable.[3] This does not mean, however, that all that person's desires will necessarily be selfish ones. So, for instance, 'I want that my hunger be satisfied', while clearly not unselfish, is not selfish either, unless it occurs in a context where its fulfilment would interfere with the well-being of others. Moreover, the states of affairs she wants to see in the world may primarily benefit others rather than herself. She may want, for instance, that she contribute to Oxfam. Such a desire is egocentric in that her motivation is not simply that she wants to help the needy, but is rather that she wants to be able to see herself as a benefactor to the needy. Still, it is not selfish. While all selfish desires are egocentric, the converse does not hold. A desire is not a selfish one if the completion of the formula specifies some benefit to accrue to others. The self-centred may be quite prepared and indeed anxious to, for

---

[3] 'Egoism and Altruism', in *Problems of the Self* (Cambridge: Cambridge University Press, 1973), 260–1: 'All the egoist's wants are either of the form "I want that I . . ." . . . or else . . . they depend on another desire which is of that form . . .'

example, show concern for and generosity towards others, and may quite correctly express their desires to others and themselves in the non-I propositional form, 'I want that so-and-so be helped'. But since the assumption is that we have here an agent whose self-consciousness is wholly explicit, this overtly non-I desire will depend on some more basic I-desire, in the sense that it would not have occurred had there not been a desire of the form, 'I want that I (can impress others with my generosity, can think of myself as being generous, can think of myself as having brought about this happy state of affairs)'. Egocentrics of this sort show concern for others, and may indeed take a great deal of trouble and sacrifice comfort or pleasure in their helpfulness to others, and so the 'selfish' label does not apply to them. Whether or not the self-centred are also selfish will depend on how they wish to see themselves as agents in the world. But whether selfish or not, neither type can have what Williams calls 'basic non-I desires', i.e. desires which do not depend on any I-desire at all, at whatever level. Basic non-I desires are only for those whose self-consciousness is implicit. It does not, however, follow that the implicitly self-conscious must therefore be morally admirable. They may indeed be saints who selflessly devote themselves to others, but just as self-centredness need not be accompanied by selfishness, so self-oblivion does not itself guarantee altruism. The latter may be wholly indifferent towards others, being devoted, perhaps, to some not necessarily worthy cause. It hardly needs saying that whether an agent acts on non-I or on non-basic I-desires is often obscure and impossible to settle either by the disinterested observer or by self-analytical probing. The generous donation may be prompted by the wish that the recipient should flourish or that the donor should be the means of his flourishing, or, perhaps most likely, by a mixture of the two.

The distinction between types of desires just drawn may be complemented by another which cuts across it: it is between desires for some goal which can be fully specified without mentioning the conscious states of others, and those which cannot be so specified. Evidently there are very many desires where reference to others would not be in place, such as desires for food and drink. But in any normal life there will also be plenty in which specification of the desire-goal refers to other-consciousness. As in the case of the implicitly self-conscious, it does not follow that there need be virtue attached to such desires. The agent concerned may aim to trivialize or harm. The better informed he is about the other's state of consciousness, the better will he know how to give pain. Mental cruelty, to be successful, relies on such knowledge. Nor need the wholly selfish be without such desires, for reference to another state of consciousness may be necessary to specify her goal of self-satisfaction. Her goal may be that she profit from the other's state of happiness, or that she manage to escape from the effects of his state of misery. Possession of desires which do refer to other-consciousness do no more than open the possibility of proper communication with others. In the present context a particularly relevant desire is to be acquainted with another's reactions to one's own attitude and behaviour. The self-centred benefactor, for example, may well wish to be assured that others appreciate what she does, and the envious are at least likely to desire from others either sympathy or a positive response to their apparently non-defective selves. But whatever their purpose, desires directed towards another's consciousness require a degree of imagination, absent, perhaps, in the wholly brutal. Of course, distinctions here, as in earlier cases, become blurred in that there will be ranges of instances where it will hardly be possible to settle which type of desire is being exhibited: a case of totally misperceived other-consciousness may approach that of lack of reference to other-consciousness altogether.

Evaluations and decisions about what it is worthwhile to do and what to avoid are clearly influenced by the kind of self-consciousness and the nature of the desires of the person concerned. They are causally operative constituents of what is her self. The degree of her own awareness of these constituents will vary across persons, and also vary across different stages of one person's development. Her view of herself may be more or less well thought out and articulate, or it may be expressed in behaviour and affective reaction rather than in speech or thought. A person's consciousness of herself may be quite inarticulate in that she does not spell out at all to either others or herself the nature of her outlook and desires, or it may be only superficially articulate, if she does not make clear to herself the implications of what she thinks and does. In this latter case she would be akin to those earlier described as 'shallowly sincere'. In some cases (and this applies to all the vicious) a high degree of articulateness is, from the agent's point of view, best avoided. The more self-centred a person is, the less likely, perhaps, that she is inclined to probe her position. Self-disguise would here be particularly easy for those whose individual desires are not patently self-referential so that they can see themselves as heroes or benefactors, as the case may be. The self-oblivious, on the other hand, can hardly spell out their basic position to themselves without spoiling that position. The problem of the highly articulate saint, therefore, is the constant worry that their other-regarding concerns might basically be a form of self-indulgence (see Ch. 5).

Another crucial feature in that complex of thoughts, desires, and evaluations constitutive of the self are the agent's feelings. Psychic feelings are of course complex in themselves in that they have various dimensions: they differ in their nature, their force, the type of object they take, if any, and in their relations to the thoughts and desires of the agent. Broadly, they may be positive or negative, where the former include not merely such obvious ones as pleasure, elation, or happiness, but also, for instance, interest and sympathy; and the negative ones comprise as well as pain and depression all sorts of hostile feelings towards others, oneself, or the world in general. The degree of either type of feeling will influence the thoughts and behaviour of the agent, whether or not she is aware of what she feels. Desires and reasoning may be more or less feeling-laden, and differences in this respect will be reflected in the degree of a person's commitments and identifications.

In his paper 'Psychic Feelings'[4] Michael Stocker distinguishes between three types of such feelings. There are, first, feelings which are objectless and primarily characterize the psyche, for example being excited, full of mental energy, having high spirits, being depressed. The second and third type both take objects and so go beyond the psyche; in a sense they are about the world. The two types are distinguished from one another in the manner in which they relate to the world. The first of these is allied to ways of seeing the world, seeing it with interest or excitedly, for example. Feelings in the final category refer to the world as the individual takes it to be;

---

[4] 'Psychic Feelings', *Australasian Journal of Philosophy* 61 1 (March 1983), 5–26.

they are allied to perceptions of how, in her view, the world actually
is. She sees that it is, for example, interesting or exciting. These distinctions go beyond what was said in an earlier chapter
about moods and emotions. They indicate a progression towards
relative objectivity. The objectivity is 'relative' in that it operates
within the subjective realm of the agent's viewpoint, but within this
perspective such a distinction can validly be drawn. Relevant here
are the two kinds of feeling which take objects: those whose being
'about' the world was connected with ways of seeing the world, and
those which seemed to be 'in' the world. It is rather misleading to
refer to them as being 'kinds' of feelings, for they do not fall into
two distinctive categories. The crucial difference is not in the specific
feelings themselves, but in how they are experienced. In the first case
it is the manner of feeling or perceiving which is characterized as
'being about the world'. Here such states of feeling or perception
are to be explained primarily by reference to other psychic states or
attitudes of the agent herself: I fear the dog and experience this bit of
the world as dangerous because I am suspicious of all dogs and think
they cannot be trusted. Or again, I am bored by the book I am reading
because I do not care for romantic literature. This state is contrasted
with that where 'in the world' is felt or perceived to characterize the
object of the feeling or perception, and here the explanation of the
state is by reference to the relevant bit of the world: I am afraid of
the dog because it has been trained as a watchdog, I am bored by
the book because the plot is feeble and the characters ill-drawn. The
agent herself may explain her present attitude in either of these ways,
but only in the latter case will she commit herself to thinking it to
be objectively grounded. Whether or not she is justified in thinking
this will depend on whether what she perceives as good reasons for
her attitude are so in fact, and this means minimally that she must
be open to possibly contrary evidence and reasons offered from a
different point of view. Failing this, it is at least doubtful that her
feeling is correctly to be explained by reference to the world rather
than in terms of other attitudes and states of her own. It may also be
the case that she herself is often or even altogether unable to see the
distinction between the two types of differently grounded feelings,
and feel to be in the world whatever is her way of experiencing it.
Instances of stubborn prejudice often exhibit failure to perceive the

difference. So did some of the slothful: being frequently bored they perceived each object of their feeling to be totally uninteresting, and did not ever see its lack of interest in their own way of seeing it. Consequently, it did not occur to them that they might be able to try and change their attitude. Persistently reading one's feelings into the world is clearly not a wise or prudent undertaking.

It is hardly possible to envisage the case of someone who, conversely, does not experience at all the more objective type of feeling, for whom 'being in the world' never qualifies the object of their feelings and perceptions, who never sees bits of the world to be exciting or dull, as deserving sympathy or horror. For her the feelings which are 'about' the world merely qualify her way of seeing the world. The perspective of agents of this sort is clearly not anchored in the world at all. This has the implication that they cannot properly assess the situation confronting them, and so cannot have proper reasons for their decisions. Such decisions as they do make can only be made on the basis of subjective preferences and aversions, which may be short-lived and arbitrary. It looks as if in this case the 'self' will collapse into something like a bundle of perceptions, with no substantial connections between them. But maybe this is too hasty a conclusion; maybe subjective states can be more established and longer-lasting than this picture presents them as being, and so, perhaps, they can afford the grounds for sufficiently good reasons on which to base decisions, and can therefore provide sufficient stability and coherence for selfhood to be possible. This suggestion does not, however, solve the difficulty. It does not do so because in the circumstances envisaged the agent's decision-procedure would hardly be intelligible, even, or perhaps particularly, to the agent herself. In forming intentions and making decisions the agent deliberates about what it would be most worthwhile for her to do; she has an interest in getting this 'right'. But what is to be her criterion here if she cannot perceive different parts of the world to be fearful or harmless, enjoyable or disturbing? The attempt to get one's decisions right would seem to require reference to some objective backing. Maybe she remembers that in the past she saw certain situations as, for example, interesting, and others as dull, and so takes these previous experiences as her guide. But in the past, too, the interest or dullness was conceived as being in her way of seeing the situation, and this does not provide her with good reason for expecting her reactions to be similar today or tomorrow. If they turn out to be the same, then this will be so only by chance, and her whole system of evaluations is insecure and unreliable. Moreover, she will not be able to assess her own desires as being more or less worth pursuing, for again there is no relatively objective means of settling the matter. All she can be guided by are her own subjective states. In such a situation there would then be no reason for not acting as one's strongest preferences prompt one to act, and the agent concerned would never have to face the situation where strong feelings incline her to act one way, but good reasons suggest that she should take another. A whole dimension of practical reasoning would disappear. In such circumstances it is doubtful whether the person can be said to be able to evaluate at all. These considerations will be seen to be relevant to some cases of vicious pride (see Ch. 5): just as some of the slothful were unable to assess properly their own situation because they failed to consider the possibility that how the world appeared to them might be alterable by a shift of view, so will the wholly arrogant be incapable of such self-assessments since, conversely, it is only their manner of viewing the world which guides them.

It is not surprising that this agent's way of proceeding has the wrong 'feel' about it: in practical deliberations agents do not think of themselves as giving expression to merely their (broadly) likes and dislikes, to be backed up by no more than further likes and dislikes. They think of at least the more important and life-guiding of the goals they aim at as being desirable (prudent, moral, enriching) quite independently of their desiring them, and do not envisage their desirability to vanish simply because their own desires change. Sisyphus, condemned by the gods to spend his life pushing a stone up a hill from where it will roll down to be pushed up again, and so on, endlessly, would no doubt have cause to be grateful if in their mercy the gods implanted in him the desire to engage in precisely this activity.[5] But he would not be in a position to consider whether or not this is a worthwhile desire to act upon. He would lack what Frankfurt has called 'second-order volitions' and lacking them would be 'a

---

[5]   This case is discussed by David Wiggins in 'Truth, Invention and the Meaning of Life', *Proceedings of the British Academy* 62 (1971), repr. in *Needs, Values, Truth* (Oxford: Basil Blackwell, 1987).

wanton'.[6] The implications are that if Sisyphus were to experience also other, conflicting desires, he would be unable to care which of them resulted in action. Of course, he may think that perpetually rolling stones an activity which yielded more pleasure than any other he could think of, but he could not conceive of the experience of pleasure as a good, let alone as the good to be achieved in life. Most importantly, he could not distinguish between those occasions when he felt in control of what he was doing, and those when he felt himself to be at the mercy of his desires. The person who struggles to, say, resist the tempting meal because he thinks it bad for his health, will, if he abstains, think of himself as having exercised his will effectively, and so as being in control of the situation. Conversely, he will appear to himself a helpless victim of his desires if he fails. Such notions of the will's success or failure are not available to someone who cannot care which of his desires he acts on. He cannot think of himself as being either strong- or weak-willed. But this means that he cannot think of himself as being an agent at all, for a person's agency reveals itself to him by the at least occasional experience of control, which manifests itself most pointedly when he does what he believes to be prudent or right in opposition to desires pulling him in a different direction. As Frankfurt says, the wanton lacks free will by default. Reduction of evaluations to mere likes and dislikes has therefore far-reaching implications: not only does it threaten to undermine the agent's ability to impose a degree of coherence on his life; it also interferes with his view of himself as being an agent at all.

If feelings are considered as merely characterizing the psyche itself or a way of seeing the world, then it is quite understandable that Kant was so firmly opposed to moral agency being based on feelings, and was so insistent on the central role of will and reason. Judgements based on wholly subjective states can hardly be taken seriously from a moral point of view. Kant's remedy was of course the extreme one of excluding feelings altogether, a move which is unavoidable only if feelings are thought to be altogether non-cognitive and cut

---

[6] Harry Frankfurt, 'Freedom of the Will and the Concept of a Person', *Journal of Philosophy*, 68 (1971), repr. in *The Importance of What We Care About* (Cambridge: Cambridge University Press, 1988). See also Charles Taylor, 'What is Human Agency?', in Theodore Mischel (ed.), *The Self* (Oxford: Basil Blackwell, 1977).

off from any possible objectivity. Consideration of the distinctions between types of feeling shows this view to be mistaken. But it shows also that Kant had a crucial point in stressing the importance of the will, of reason and objectivity. Feelings and perceptions that some bit of the world has a certain quality and so is, or is not, worth engaging with, provide the agent with the possibility of referring to publicly accessible and so assessable reasons for her choice. This in turn means that there is the possibility of discussion with others, and the consequent possibility of reassessment and a change of mind. Lacking these possibilities, the 'wanton' will hardly be able to communicate with them. She can let them know her wishes but cannot begin to defend or justify them. For the same reason others will remain a mystery to her, for she will not be able to grasp their practical deliberations. This failure in communication will throw further doubt on her ability to evaluate at all.

The conclusion to be drawn is that total failure to perceive or feel the world as having or lacking features which are attractive or valuable drastically affects the nature of the self and its relationship with others. Those concerned are not intelligible to either themselves or others. Their defect may be seen in different ways. They may, as on the Frankfurt model, be said to lack that type of will which is necessary for agency. Lacking this, they also lack a rational decision-procedure, for explaining preferred choices simply by reference to further preferences is ultimately not adequate. For although, for example, 'it gives me pleasure' may be a perfectly good reason for action on many occasions, there are also many others when it needs defending. Pleasure needs to be assessed in comparison with other values, and this the wanton cannot do. But proper decision-procedures must involve such considerations, and consequently those to whom they are not available cannot be said properly to engage in practical reasoning at all. And this will lead to the conclusion that in their lack of rationality they are thereby also defective as agents.

The same conclusion will be reached if the defect is seen as a failure properly to evaluate the choices on offer. Preferences are to be distinguished from evaluations in at least these respects:[7] evaluations

---

[7] Alternatively, if preferences are thought of as evaluations, then the distinction is between strong and weak evaluations. See Taylor, ibid.

are relatively long-lived while preferences may be fleeting, and unlike preferences they cannot be lightly dismissed or changed. This implies that they are reason-backed, even if the reason is not clear to the agent. At least she will feel her evaluations as important and worthwhile, and not at the mercy of fleeting desires. In her own view, she should be guided by her evaluations on those occasions when they conflict with mere preferences. That will be the 'right' thing to do, and expressing herself in terms of 'right' and 'wrong' implies a reference to some relatively objective standard. So even if she cannot spell out her reasons for the assessment, she will think that there are such reasons. It is because evaluations are seen as involving more than purely subjective states that they can provide on the one hand a point and a stability to decision-making which preferences alone cannot provide; and on the other enable the agent to discuss with others her opinions about the world. Her attempts to defend and justify her evaluations will involve referring to something which she believes the other will also recognize as a value or disvalue. But those who do not feel bits of the world to have properties which make it worthwhile to engage with or avoid, rely on preferences and aversions only. So they are not evaluators, and this makes them defective as practical reasoners, and so also defective as agents.

The cases envisaged have of course been unrealistically extreme in postulating a total lack of feeling that certain qualities are in the world, or conversely, a total projection onto the world of all feelings which take an object. The distinction between the two kinds of feeling under discussion is often not easy to see by perfectly normal agents, and it may indeed not be clear that in certain cases such a distinction can sensibly be drawn. This is one reason why ethical issues tend to be so problematic. The vicious, however, are confused in areas where it would be possible to take a clearer view, but their confusion is so deep-rooted a conviction that it cannot be shaken by rational considerations. Theirs may be the situation already mentioned: they believe that what qualifies their way of seeing the world is in fact a quality in the world, and so, in their view, what they believe is evidently true, and so, of course, is not open to counter-arguments. Molière's miser, for instance, takes it to be an indisputable fact that everyone around him is grasping and greedy. Alternatively, they may misguidedly take their preferences to be evaluations, and so believe themselves to have good reasons and be perfectly rational in their choices. Thus the desire to destroy the owner of the coveted good may present itself as a perfectly rational one to the envious.

Feelings are among the mental constituents which make the person what she is. They influence, perhaps determine, evaluations. Sincere evaluations, while needing some relatively objective reference, are embedded in feelings. Where they are not so grounded any sincerity will be shallow in that it is not fully assented to. The agent may conceivably be aware of this state. So, for instance, Querry's charitable actions were in this sense shallow, and knowing this contributed to his depression. In other cases the agent may himself not fully realize or turn away from his shallowness, and let himself be taken in by transitory feelings of conviction. Here is one form of self-deception, one way in which his mental states do not cohere.

We have come across other possible candidates for self-deception, namely, the confusion between preferences and evaluation, and the inclination to accept as being in the world what may be merely a way of seeing it. Self-deception is analogous to self-knowledge in that in neither case does it consist in beliefs, false in one case and true in the other, about some one entity, for the self is not such an entity. Neither self-deception nor self-knowledge is *of* anything. It is true that one can form beliefs about oneself based on attention to one's own thoughts and reactions, and that one may be right or wrong in one's conclusions based on these. This approach to oneself is similar to that which one may adopt towards others. But it does not go to the heart of the matter, for it sidesteps what is essential to the self, namely the self-creating process and the deliberations and decision-makings that involves. Self-knowledge and self-deception depend on this process being in the 'right' or 'wrong' direction respectively. Both have degrees, and neither is ever complete in the sense that it can be recorded as settled and done with, for they themselves are part of the process. Those who are gaining in self-knowledge will become clearer as to what their values are and what they really want from life, and this will be a reliable basis for future decisions. Those who get involved in self-deception will on the contrary be confused about their values and their wants. Both, knowledge and deception, will tend to be self-perpetuating, and, since they are part of the self-creating process, both can be said to be *in* rather than of the self.[8]

The agent who has self-knowledge tends to be described as being 'true to herself' or 'authentic'. The self-deceptive agent, by contrast, creates a 'false self'. The criterion for 'falsity' (as for 'truth') is in the agents themselves. Where self-deception is persistent and ever self-perpetuating their most centrally important wants will be incoherent. The incoherence may be in their overriding aim itself. This was so for the avaricious; fulfilment of their basic desires was doomed from the start. Or there may be an inconsistency between their most deeply embedded overall desire and the means they adopt towards its fulfilment. This was the case of the viciously envious, whose aim of creating an esteem-worthy self could not be achieved by the means they saw fit to adopt.

Incoherence among desires reflects incoherence in assessment of the worthwhile. The vicious do not know what their most central 'real' wants, or convictions, are. Convictions require both: that they be embedded in the agent's feelings, and that the assessments involved be by the agent believed to be true, and not thought merely to rest on other feelings of hers. These two elements support each other: if the belief is shaken the emotional attachment will tend to weaken, though that may take some time, since feelings tend to be slow in following cognitive insight. Weakening in feelings means that the belief in the truth of the assessment is now not strongly held and will, therefore, be easier to dislodge. So it may come to be abandoned and seen merely as a prejudice. Since it is no longer a part of the agent's wider system of feelings and assessments it will lack the coherence which supported the belief in its truth.

Negatively, the interconnection between feeling and belief was seen in the shallowly sincere. Their belief in the truth of their assessment may well outlive their 'sincerity', but if so it will be a wholly intellectual or theoretical belief, and consequently not play any significant part in their practical lives. The reason for the sincerity

---

[8] Ilham Dilman discusses the connection between self-knowledge and moral agency in 'Self-Knowledge and the Reality of Good and Evil', in Raymond Gaita (ed.), *Value and Understanding: Festschrift in Honour of Peter Winch* (London: Routledge, 1990). For a discussion of different kinds of self-knowledge, see Hamlyn, 'Self-Knowledge'.

being 'shallow' was that their evaluations were not grounded in their feelings. Consequently, theirs was no conviction but was merely a transitory feeling of conviction. Insincerity operates in the opposite direction; it is exhibited by those whose belief in the truth of the assessment is based on the desire that it be truth. If this is the belief's foundation, then the agent cannot afford to put it to the test. On the contrary, it had better not be exposed, for that might reveal its falsity. So the agent, as it were, compensates by strengthening the feeling part of the conviction, and thus clings more and more to the belief. Here the feeling of conviction is not transitory but is deeply embedded. It is protected from any more impartial attack. This is an imbalance which is characteristic of the vicious. In this sense there is truth in the traditional view that the vicious are guided by passion rather than reason, that their faculties are not in harmony.

Self-deception inevitably spreads. At least it does so where it occurs in the area of central wants and assessments, as it does in the case of the vicious. Because they have to protect their feelings of conviction these have to become ever more embedded in their whole system of feelings and thoughts, to achieve the kind of coherence which, in the false self, is the analogue to the coherence attained by those whose beliefs in the truth of their assessments is well supported. The protection is against others who may challenge the relevant beliefs. But most importantly it is the agents themselves who have to be protected from self-discovery. So they need to be doubly protected, to be achieved by embedding their feelings of conviction as securely as possible, thus making it ever harder for themselves to abandon the deception in the self. Both the avaricious and the envious may be said to devote much effort to ever greater protection of a false self.

The slothful alone of the vicious may not be self-deceptive, though under certain circumstances they will be shallowly sincere. They, therefore, cannot be described as protecting a false self. But this is not surprising: they are not engaged with either the world or with themselves. Although the focus of their attention is their own selves, this is not an interested attention. Since there is no engagement there is no proper evaluation, either, and so they are not in a position even to misevaluate. In their case there is no sufficiently developed self to be either true or false.

Self-deception is self-protective. There is, from the agent's point of view, some (in central cases, great) advantage to be gained. It is understandable that, since recognition of a self as false would set in trail enormous upheavals, it should appear well worth avoiding. But why create a false self in the first place? This creation, too, is a protection, and so the agents concerned must see a need for protection, and consequently must see themselves as being threatened in some way. The centrally and deeply self-deceptive cannot act out of conviction but act out of feelings of conviction which need to be nourished by some strong feeling or feelings. The emotional reaction to threats is fear, and this would seem to be what prompts the self-deceptive. Since fear tends to cloud one's judgements it would explain their failure to evaluate properly, and since fear tends to undermine one's control of a situation, it would explain also their defects as proper agents. The vicious discussed so far fit this picture. This is quite plain in the case of the miserly avaricious, who are in the grip of an overriding desire for security. The envious, too, are anxious: they fear for their standing, fear that they cannot achieve a worthwhile position by their own efforts. The slothful, whether or not they are shallowly sincere, seem to be afraid of tackling life at all. It remains to be seen to what extent the remaining vices conform to this pattern.

5 PRIDE AND ANGER

I

OF all the vices examined here, pride is the one which most patently involves consciousness of self and self-evaluation. The assessment of its nature and implicit harm will depend on the features of the self set out in the last chapter.

There are different types of pride and, as in the case of envy, not all of them are corruptive. Hume, for example, thought it 'evident' that pride is not always vicious, and it has often been praised as a virtue.[1] But it has also been labelled the deadliest of the deadly sins. So it has been regarded as both a wholly desirable virtue and a thoroughly destructive vice. For my purposes the field can be narrowed. Since my concern is with a person's possession of a vice, the relevant characterization of pride will refer to that person's embedded state of mind, or attitude, and not apply to moods or emotions occurring only occasionally. Feeling proud of this or that on some specific occasion may well be quite harmless or even beneficial to those who experience the emotion, and it is this case Hume has in mind when he thinks it so obvious that pride is not always vicious. He is right, I think, in claiming that the 'agreeable passion of pride' is always ultimately a feeling of self-applause, of esteem for oneself as, for example, the owner of a beautiful house, or as the parent of successful children. Feelings of pride ultimately focus on the self, with agreeable interest, as Hume suggests. The sight or thought of my beautiful house is

---

[1] *A Treatise of Human Nature*, bk. 2, pt. 1, sect. 7. According to Aristotle, the kind of pride which is magnanimity is a virtue; *Nicomachean Ethics*, 1123^{a}31–^{b}13. Also Aquinas, *Summa Theologiae* (*ST*) 2a2ae q. 129 art. 3. For a recent account see John Casey, *Pagan Virtue* (Oxford: Oxford University Press, 1992), ch. 1, para. 6.

the occasion for thinking of myself with some pleasure as the owner of that house. Self-consciousness in this as in all types of pride is explicit, focused on the agent herself in this or that capacity. But such emotions may be short-lived and have no repercussions on the person's view of her overall standing. While sharing some features with other manifestations of pride, emotional pride of this sort is not directly relevant to pride thought of as either virtue or vice, and therefore will be set aside.

Hume is also among those who regarded pride as a virtue (*Treatise of Human Nature*, bk. 3, pt. 3, sect. 2), for, he thought, pride expresses a due sense of our own force and so amounts to proper self-esteem. Pride so understood is also set aside for the time being. Hume agrees, however, that pride may go wrong and express itself as 'overweening conceit'. Such conceit, he thinks, is not to be recommended since it is disagreeable to others who do not care to be looked down upon. So Hume agrees that pride may be vicious, but does so on the grounds of its ill-effect on others, rather than on the agent herself. But the present concern is with the harm the vicious inflict upon themselves, so it is from this latter point of view that the potentially vicious types of pride are to be examined here. At least three main types may be distinguished; they are vanity, conceit, and arrogance. Each of these types covers a wide range of cases, and any individual who is vain, conceited, or arrogant will of course be so to a greater or lesser degree. The cases considered here are, as before, of characters whose perspective on life is assumed to be wholly coloured by the relevant form of pride. Vanity and conceit are introduced largely to distinguish them from arrogance, the type of pride which, I think, is the deadliest. But of course all three forms have features in common.

The dominant feature of a wholly vain person is her absorbing concern with her appearance. Interest in how she appears is interest in the effect she has on others. Appearance may diverge from 'reality', whatever that may be, and being merely appearance remain on the surface. Where there is such a gap the vain will tend to spend much time and energy on an appearance which is designed to hide from others and also from herself the less acceptable reality. Most obviously, though not necessarily, it is the person's physical appearance which is the focus of her attention and care. A comic version of this obvious type is personified in Dickens's Mrs Skewton

(*Dombey and Son*, ch. 21). Aged about seventy, she dresses in a fashion that would have been youthful for a woman of twenty-seven. She fancies herself a Cleopatra, and to keep up the appearance lets herself be pushed in a wheelchair where she can maintain the pose in which she was once—fifty years earlier—painted by a fashionable artist 'who had appended to his published sketch the name of Cleopatra'. But when Mrs Skewton is being prepared for the night, 'the painted object shrivelled . . . an old, worn, yellow, nodding woman, with red eyes, alone remained in Cleopatra's place . . .' (ch. 27).

Mrs Skewton means to direct the attention of others, and through them her own, away from the real state of affairs. She needs to be reassured about her physical appearance and youthfulness, and seeks such reassurance even though she can hardly escape the knowledge that she is no longer a young and attractive woman. But while in this type of case appearance (or at any rate appearance as envisaged by the agent) does not at all correspond to reality, there is also the type of the truly beautiful who are vain of this beauty. In George Eliot's *Middlemarch*, for example, the narrator remarks of the acknowledged beauty, Rosamond Vincy, that her every nerve and muscle was adjusted to the consciousness that she was being looked at (ch. 12). Here there is no divergence between physical appearance as presented to the world and as it really is. But Mrs Skewton and Rosamond are alike in attaching vital importance to this appearance and the impression that is to make on others. They are concerned above all with the picture they present to the world; they offer their appearance as a means of attracting praise and applause, which they in turn can respond to with heightened self-esteem. The vain offer their appearance as a means of seducing others into thinking well of them, which in turn is a means of seducing themselves to think well of themselves.[2]

Such an attitude is not that of a person who is secure in her self-esteem. On the contrary, she seeks to find her own value in the judgement of others. She therefore will tend to take pleasure in every favourable opinion about herself which she can gather, and be

---

[2] Nietzsche has a point when he speaks of the vain as being slavish in their attitude: *Beyond Good and Evil* (Oxford: Oxford University Press, 1999), para. 261. See also Casey, *Pagan Virtue*, ch. 1, para. 6.

depressed by any adverse one, quite regardless of its appropriateness or truth. She clings to the opinions of others since on these hinges her self-evaluation. But this leaves her in a precarious position, for the response of others is hardly something to be relied upon, especially if what satisfies the vain is flattery rather than honest conviction. Others may not wish to play the game, may change their minds, and so on. Spinoza comments on what he calls 'empty honour', the self-approval 'fostered only by the good opinion of the populace': 'he whose honour is rooted in popular approval must, day by day, anxiously strive, act and scheme in order to retain his reputation. For the populace is variable and inconstant . . .'[3] The 'populace' may indeed be fickle and unreliable, and awareness of such instability will lead to anxiety on the part of the vain, which in turn will tend to encourage them to give yet more attention to their appearance to the world and the seduction of the opinion of others, and so it seems that all their effort cannot be crowned with lasting success. And further, in their constant search for a specific response the vain see others as merely a potential audience from whom admiration can be extracted, a view which must rule out the possibility of entering into proper personal relationships.

The wholly vain plainly exhibit central features which resemble those of the vicious already discussed: they are insecure in their self-evaluation, and to compensate look for a shallow substitute which cannot provide what they need, and cannot allay their anxiety. Their overriding desire, to gain esteem through presenting the 'right' appearance, makes them akin to the envious in that the means they adopt towards fulfilling this desire cannot provide what they are looking for.

The conceited closely resemble the vain in that they, too, depend on others to sustain the conviction of their own excellence, but they differ in the nature of their dependence. While the vain need others to reflect a flattering image of themselves, the conceited use them as that against which their own superiority may be measured. Hume's 'overweening conceit', which was so disagreeable to those made to feel despised, clearly implied a comparison with others which always

---

[3] B. Spinoza, *The Ethics*, pt. 4, proposition 58.

worked to the comparer's own advantage. This outcome of the comparison is not an unexpected one: the conceited look at another precisely in order to find in her inferiority confirmation of their own superiority. In this their perspective is the converse of that of the envious, who always saw others to be in a position which was better than their own. In contrast to the envious, the self-esteem of the conceited seems confirmed by the comparison, which consequently would appear to benefit them. On the other hand, the need to take such a perspective on life, to be preoccupied with looking out for support, is evidently suspect: a self-esteem requiring constant reassurance can hardly be secure. It is a sham self-esteem. This was equally true of those who are vain, but their case is the more complex one. The spotting of inferiority in others is after all a fairly crude way of attempting to shine. The vain, on the other hand, play around with substitutions. They substitute the apparent for the real, the superficial for the weighty, both in their self-image and in their demands on others.

Kant, in his lecture on Haughtiness, distinguishes between haughtiness (*Hochmut*) and arrogance (*Stolz*). Haughtiness is conceit in that it 'feels itself superior to others and undervalues them'. Arrogance, however, does not involve comparison: it is 'the pride which pretends to an importance which it does not possess'. As a form of pride it naturally shares certain crucial features with vanity and conceit, but it also has a further characteristic which sets it apart from these and makes it the more deadly: it is wholly self-referential. Like the vain, the arrogant substitute illusion for reality, but unlike them they are indifferent to admiration and approval from others. Their self-esteem need not be nourished in either this way or by comparison. All forms of pride concern the relation between self and other. Vanity and conceit are vicious in that, in different ways, they falsify this relation, and in doing so they attach an importance to their own position which is quite out of proportion with that which they attach to others, whose role it is merely to serve their needs. But others could not fulfil this role if at least in this respect they were not taken seriously. Hence in their reliance on others the vain and conceited at least acknowledge their coexistence. The arrogantly proud, however, do not seem to need any such support from others. They rather see themselves as being on a different plane, as being superior and unique. The referend of the personal pronoun 'I' is, in their view, a different sort of being from that which is indicated by 'you' or 'they'. This makes them moral solipsists and—as the other side of the coin—moral sceptics about other minds. Their solipsism and scepticism are 'moral' because they concern the ascription of needs, rights, and values to the agent and to others respectively. Shakespeare's Coriolanus may be taken to provide a relevant paradigm case.

Coriolanus seems to show admirable integrity when he refuses to flatter the people of Rome so that they vote for him to become Consul. Flattery involves dishonesty, and dishonesty he sees as a form of cowardice. But Coriolanus is a hero and so has nothing but contempt for anything that hints at cowardice. He will not stoop to work dishonestly for his own advantage. And he is right in thinking that the conventions governing the election demand a degree of wooing of the people which might well be thought insincere and demeaning. It turns out, however, that what Coriolanus sees as a demand for flattery on the part of the citizens includes the demand that their needs be appreciated and their rights acknowledged. Since, in his view, the people are of no account and not worthy of having rights, to accede to such demands is itself a piece of unwarranted flattery. It is true that the citizens are mutinous and their behaviour hardly admirable, but this is not the point: it is not, or not merely, on empirical grounds that he despises them. They are scum and as such, it appears from his first meeting with them, not worthy even of being treated civilly:

> What's the matter, you dissentious rogues
> That, rubbing the poor itch of your opinion,
> Make yourselves scabs? (I. i. 162)

Coriolanus's view of flattery in this case is itself an expression of his deeply ingrained anti-democratic political convictions. Ordinary citizens are not to be thought of in the same terms as he is himself, and as are others of his class. But while in his relation to the citizens he is overbearing and arrogant, he can hardly be thought a moral solipsist for he still sees himself as belonging to a community the members of which have equal rights, and with whom it is possible to communicate. At least, it looks as if he is a member of a value-sharing community, but it is clear that other patricians, including his mother

Volumnia, have no conception of what he means by 'honour', and what for him honourable behaviour must imply. Coriolanus sees them as (possible) equals only as long as things go his own way. When the patricians fail to prevent his banishment, that is, fail to treat him as, in his view, he deserves, they, by making common cause with the scum, have lost class, honour, and rights. They are 'ingrates' and 'dastards' with whom it would be dishonourable to identify. On the contrary, to right his own position they have to be crushed. So he plans the burning of Rome.

Coriolanus never questions for a moment that his view of the situation is correct, that every step he takes is fully justified, and is indeed required of a man of honour. 'I banish you' he says to Rome when he is exiled. Roman virtue, it seems, rests with him alone; other possible bearers have shown themselves to be unworthy. As he sees it, his in all respects superior position generates an honour-code which determines who is allowed to share his universe. Others, therefore, exist as persons only on sufferance; they are expelled as soon as they fail his expectations. The implication is that he sees himself as the only stable occupier of this universe; the presence of others is merely a contingent one, depending on his will.

Coriolanus is alienated from all others; he is quite isolated. Both he and others emphasize this point: 'Alone I fought in Corioles walls' (I. viii. 8); 'Alone I did it' (V. vi. 117); 'He has no equal' (I. i. 251). His status is compared to that of a god, again by both himself and others: he means to behave 'as if man were author of himself and knew no other kin' (V. iii. 36); and it is said of him: 'He wants nothing of a god but eternity and a heaven to throne in' (V. iv. 23). His isolation is typical of the arrogantly proud; it is the consequence of their thinking themselves godlike. To see its nature and implications we have to look at the form of self-consciousness involved.

All the viciously proud are wholly self-centred; their view of the world is the view of themselves in the world. But, as was pointed out in the last chapter, such explicit self-consciousness may be more or less 'directly' so; the 'I-desires' it involves may or may not be basic. At one extreme explicit self-consciousness is quite patent, focusing directly on the self-image, as does Narcissus admiring his reflection in the water. At the other extreme the concentration on the self is so indirect that the distinction between implicit and explicit self-consciousness becomes blurred. In between these extremes the self-consciousness of the proud is to various degrees directly or indirectly focused on the self. They may have outgoing interests, even appear to be wholly dedicated to some worldly or spiritual cause. Coriolanus, for example, has many desires which appear to be non-I desires: he is interested in the fighting of wars, affairs of state, and proper government, and in having these he is not selfish. But he and other arrogantly proud are self-centred nonetheless, for in their case such desires are reducible to basic I-desires in that what they desire above all is to see themselves as, for instance, the heroic soldier or brilliant administrator. Ultimately their other-regarding concerns are means merely towards serving their own superior status.

The variety within this type of self-consciousness accounts not only for the variety in cases of arrogant pride, but also for the difficulty in assessing motivation, both on the part of others and on that of the agent himself. Particularly at risk are those whose way of life sets them apart from people leading ordinary lives, namely, the heroes, saints, and martyrs. They may strike others as being sinfully proud, and may themselves wonder whether their dedication to a cause is a means to self-admiration rather than an end in itself. Thomas Becket as characterized by his attackers in T. S. Eliot's *Murder in the Cathedral* would be a case in point: far from being saintly, they think, he is bent on spiritual self-glorification. If we accept this view of him then Becket's self-consciousness was wholly explicit, presumably indirectly so:

> His pride always feeding upon his own virtues,
> Pride drawing sustenance from impartiality,
> Pride drawing sustenance from generosity,
> Loathing power given by temporal devolution
> Wishing subjection to God alone.   (Part I)

On such a reading, Thomas's impartial and generous actions and his subjection to God will veil his pride and allow him to delude himself.

But even where a person's self-consciousness is directly explicit, he need not make it clear to himself that this is so. For cutting across the explicit/implicit distinction was the degree of the person's articulateness. This, too, had different dimensions: it could be outward or inward, showing itself in the greater or lesser ability to communicate

with others, or in being more or less self-perceptive, being able to
a greater or lesser degree to formulate clear thoughts about oneself
and one's aims. Coriolanus, it has often been noted,[4] is not particularly articulate in his communication with others. Words, in many
contexts, seem to him a vehicle for flattery. ('When blows have made
me stay, I fled from words' (II. ii). But even more striking is his inward
dumbness. There is in the play a minimal use of soliliqui. Coriolanus
is not given to reflection, he does not probe his motivation, does
not clearly formulate his aims or weigh his reasons for action. It is
ironic that Coriolanus, who insists on total honesty, on saying only
what is in one's heart, seems unable to discover precisely what is in
his heart. His inarticulateness, and the inability of other characters
to understand him, contribute to the mystification which tends to be
experienced by spectators or readers of the play; it seems impossible
to disentangle fully Coriolanus's motivation. Inarticulateness of this
sort is a feature of the arrogantly proud.[5]

The reason is that in crucial respects their language degenerates
into a private one. It is this which makes their life one of fantasy
and self-delusion. There are several aspects to this delusion: first,
the arrogantly proud think of themselves as operating with a value-
system which is superior to that of others. But this is not so; on the
contrary, the proud cannot have a proper grasp of the language of
values at all because they have no access to any form of objectivity,
and so have no criterion for discriminating between preferences and
evaluations. Of course, the proud, like everyone else, are brought up
in a community and exposed to the relevant values, which they may
accept or come to reject. At any rate it gives them a framework of
values. Coriolanus would not want to see himself as heroic soldier
or outstanding statesman if he did not, as a true patrician of his
time, think of such professions as (probably) uniquely worthy of
pursuit. So he values them. But he is wholly intolerant of both values
differing from his own, in that he will not even consider them, and

---

[4] See the collection of articles in *Shakespeare: Coriolanus*, ed. B. A. Brockman,
Casebook Series (London: Macmillan, 1977), esp. M. Charney, 'Style in the Roman
Plays'; and K. G. Hunter, 'The Last Tragic Heroes'.

[5] There is the same sort of mystification about the motivation of Ibsen's Hedda
Gabler, another character who is—among other things—arrogantly proud.

interpretations differing from his own as to what or who is to be seen as manifesting what he values. In both respects he takes himself to be the only judge. So he lives in a world apart, seeing himself as special and the centre of the universe, and so the sole arbiter on what is to be accepted as worthwhile. But without any point of reference beyond himself his evaluations collapse into preferences. This does not imply that the proud act as any old desire may prompt them to, but it does imply that the only assessment of their desires will be their own higher-order desires, the more long-standing and deep-rooted ones. This of course is always a danger in the use of value-language. But the proud refuse to test their views in any way, they do not think they have to give reasons or offer justifications, for it is given that what others think is neither here nor there, that their opinions are not worth taking notice of. The implication is not only that they are not justified in their elevation of what they value, but that, more basically, their way of using a value-term lacks all context, and consequently prevents the proud from understanding its role in a language.

Secondly, where there is no possibility of some subjective/objective distinction, there is also no possibility of having knowledge. There cannot be an appeal to any kind of truth-criteria, but such a possibility is a necessary condition for knowledge. The arrogantly proud, therefore, can have knowledge of neither others nor themselves as evaluating agents. But a person's evaluations and commitments are constitutive of that person's identity, so that knowledge of another person will entail some understanding of the values they live by. Having no shared value-structure, the proud can neither know others nor be known by them. But self-knowledge depends at least on taking seriously others' reactions to oneself and one's own reaction to others, and this the proud do not do. Finally, the lack of this possibility entails the impossibility of any self-development. In their isolation and self-absorption the proud cannot learn and profit from their learning. Their position is a wholly static one. No wonder Coriolanus is stubborn and inflexible, and his reaction to others often childish.

Given these features it is clear the proud must suffer from a shrivelled self, being deprived of interrelationships and crucial types of knowledge. The contrast is great indeed between the fantasy self and what the self has turned out to be. This, surely, is an indication that there is an inherent contradiction in their aims and desires.

The fatal flaw in the desire-structure of the proud of this type is a point raised, in a different context, by Stanley Cavell.[6] Referring to the food-imagery in *Coriolanus* he speaks of Coriolanus and Volumnia as starvers: 'They manifest this as a condition of insatiability (starving by feeding, feeding as deprivation). It is a condition sometimes described as the infiniteness of desire.' I want to try and clarify a little the paradox here referred to. For a possible illustration of this aspect of the case I turn again to the (wholly unheroic) figure of Mr Casaubon, who can be seen to be arrogant as well as a spiritual miser. His apparently all-absorbing interest is in his scholarly work, but it is clear that here we have another case of indirect explicit self-consciousness: his concern is with himself as the great scholar, and all he wants from his wife Dorothea is assistance in propping up this image. It is true, of course, that he is given a more human setting and outlook, and the scale of his arrogance can hardly be compared with that of Coriolanus. It is much more modest, so to speak, and cracks are apparent in various forms of anxieties. Perhaps because of his more manageable scale he more clearly illustrates the features Cavell appears to point to: the more Casaubon is concerned with the nature of his image, the less he can concentrate on and respond to the demands of his scholarship, for as we saw earlier (Ch. 3), while trying to protect his image he neglected relevant scholarly material. But his image is based on his scholarship, yet that is more and more defective. So that which feeds the image will diminish, and the more food he needs to feed the image the less food there is, the hungrier he gets, the more food he needs... His desire is indeed insatiable and must lead to starvation. The measure of insatiability can be seen in his attempt to try for satisfaction after his death by planning to get Dorothea to promise that she would abide by his wishes concerning his work, thus meaning her to keep on feeding his self-image when he himself is no longer able to do so.

The insatiability and hence infinity of relevant desires hinges on their self-reflexivity, on the proud's concern for the superiority and self-sufficiency of his position. The proud see themselves as gods, and

---

[6] In his complex paper '*Coriolanus* and Interpretations of Politics', in *Disowning Knowledge in Six Plays of Shakespeare* (Cambridge: Cambridge University Press, 1987), 148.

hence as perfect. Their crucial desires, then, are to have this position confirmed and maintained. But this itself raises a difficulty and shows up a paradox in their situation. It does so in two ways: first, to desire a state or thing is to want something one at present lacks. So desiring something itself expresses a lack, it is in itself an indication of a degree of dependence, it points to less than self-sufficiency. Having desires at all is therefore a difficulty for the proud. Secondly and consequently, there is a problem about the object of their desires. If the proud wish for godlike perfection and self-sufficiency then, it seems, their desire would have to be that they be desire*less*. But can one desire to be desireless? Such a desire would at any rate be insatiable since the proud, as human beings, have natural limitations which make total self-sufficiency—mental as well as physical—quite impossible. Hence approaching their case from this point of view also leads to the conclusion that they cannot have what they want. And further, Cavell asks: 'If you desire to be desireless, is there something you desire?' (p. 149). Even if there is here an object of desire it is evidently not of the kind that can be clearly characterized and explained. No wonder, then, that Coriolanus is such a poor communicator, and no wonder that he has little understanding of himself. 'Being godlike' as a description of the aim only *appears* to provide an answer, for it begs the question of what precisely it is that is wished for. The notion of a desireless self is hardly a comprehensible one. It would seem to be a self which is not engaged with the world at all, and hence a self which has lost that which gives it substantial identity. If so, the proud would be akin to the wholly slothful, who could not be regarded as agents at all. The proud, it would appear, in wishing to be godlike, desire their spiritual death.

The proud of this type are involved in a continuum of unfulfillable desires. To survive, to break out of the circle of desires, they need food from some external source, in the form of some recognition and confirmation of their self-image. But who could provide such food? It could come only from someone they regard as an equal, but in their view there is no equal, there is no one whose food is good enough. So the route to survival is barred, and self-destruction is inherent in the position of the arrogantly proud.

The vain and the conceited patently look for support for their self-image, and so it is plain that they are not sure of their position. They are involved in the process of constantly seeking reassurance of their worth through the avoidance of self-knowledge. The arrogantly proud do not seem to be in need of such reassurance. Their avoidance of dependence on others seems total and complete, and so, one might suppose, the sense of their own worth is exceptionally well established. And this indeed is as they appear. Of course, since none of their valuations can be genuine, their self-assessment cannot be taken seriously, either, but this does not mean that they may not themselves feel secure in their feelings of superiority. But if so, then only because they have created for themselves a position which is so isolated that it precludes any threat to their self-image. They have no need for reassurance only because they have already fully protected themselves by making sure that their fantasy is impregnable. Far from indicating a sense of security such moves rather point to a refusal to face at all the issue of an esteem-worthy self. Maybe this entitles the arrogantly proud to hold the position of exhibiting the deadliest of all the vices.

II

Coriolanus, that paradigm of arrogant pride, is also given to frequent bursts of anger. This is no mere coincidence. W. H. Auden speaks of the sin of anger as a reaction to a threat to the fancy that our own existence is more important than the existence of anybody else.[7] This fits the case of Coriolanus well enough: both citizens and patricians act in ways which do not appear to acknowledge his unique position, and anger is an appropriate response on his part to those who wish to thwart him. If an angry disposition is an aspect of the proud's character then this would support the suspicion that their high self-esteem is not as secure and invulnerable as it appears to be, for to be disposed to feel anger and act accordingly is to be inclined to find occasions on which another's behaviour is to be seen as insulting, since their superior status does not seem to be acknowledged. So they hit out, verbally or physically, in retaliation. But such a disposition is hardly compatible with total conviction of one's superior worth. It rather indicates some need on the proud persons' part to have their

---

[7] 'Anger', in *Seven Deadly Sins* (London: Sunday Times Publications, 1962).

view of themselves if not confirmed then at least not threatened by others, and so points to an unacknowledged dependence on others, in contradiction to their assumption of uniqueness.

The connection between pride and anger is reflected in Aristotle's discussion of the irascible, the patient, and the imperturbable.[8] In contrast to the irascible, the patient or good-natured will not experience anger at the slightest provocation, nor will they be inclined to exaggerate the number of occasions where the words or deeds of others may be seen as insulting. Their self-esteem is properly grounded, and so they need not be on constant guard against attack. On the other hand, knowing their proper worth, they will be angry with those who fail to pay them the respect which they deserve. Their patience is due not to lack of perceptiveness or insensitivity about another's attitude towards them, but rather to a rational assessment of the situation and a grasp of the importance or triviality of what is at stake. This distinguishes them not only from the irascibles' excessive anger-reaction, but also from those at the other end of the scale who never feel anger when encountering lack of respect, and who consequently cannot assert themselves and are regarded as servile. The patient react with the right degree of anger on those occasions when it is right to do so, and their anger is righteous. The servile ought to feel angry when they do not, and the irascible ought not to feel angry when they do. Both these defective reactions are the result of misguided self-evaluation, which is vastly exaggerated in the latter case, and wholly deficient in the former.[9]

The anger of Aristotle's irascible man is 'excessive' in a number of ways: it may be excessive in that it is too violent a reaction in a given situation. This is the kind of excess primarily suggested by the label 'wrath', which is sometimes used to refer to the deadly sin. The wrathful are given to bursts of temper quite out of proportion to the occasion; they lose control of themselves and so may do much

---

[8] *Nicomachean Ethics*, bk. 4, $1125^b14-1126^b10$. Both the right disposition towards anger and its deficiency, Aristotle thinks, lack a name, and 'patience' and 'imperturbability' only roughly indicate what he has in mind.

[9] Daniel H. Frank, 'Anger as a Vice: A Maimonidean Critique of Aristotle's Ethics', *History of Philosophy Quarterly* 7 (1990), 269–81, discusses the relation between self-esteem and anger in Aristotle's *Nicomachean Ethics*.

harm, both to others and to themselves. They are the angry who in Dante's *Purgatory* live in thick smoke, indicative of the lack of clarity which prevails when reason is subdued by passion. In his *Inferno* they are occupied with destroying each other. Such an extreme reaction implies that the irascible man is very conscious of possible slights, and so his anger will be excessive also in respect of the range of occasions to which he responds with this emotion; excessive, therefore, in what he regards as an insult to be taken seriously. For him the world is full of people refusing to give him the respect he considers due to him, an attitude which in turn implies that he is much concerned with the importance of his own position.

If this characterization is correct, then it seems that anger differs fundamentally from the other vices discussed. For whether or not it is vicious would seem to depend on the presence or absence of another vice, namely, that of some form of vicious pride. If so, it would not be a vice in its own right. On the other hand, a person may not necessarily be proud to react with wrath; she may just be very uncertain in her self-esteem. Aggressive anger of the type just described resembles the other deadly vices in its concern with the standing of the self and the fear that a treasured self-image may be threatened or seen to be unfounded. Such anxieties need not necessarily be based on some sort of vicious pride. Yet it is true that it is hard to see wrath as a deadly vice on its own account. This may be so partly because there may be righteous and justified anger, and because on certain occasions it may even be indicative of a defect not to feel angry. To this Aristotelean view it may be objected that in thinking it right to be feeling angry on certain occasions there is an assumption that a person's self-evaluation necessarily depends at least to a degree on the treatment received from other people, for only if this is assumed will a slight from others be potentially so harmful. But this need not be so, and is not so on, for instance, the view that self-esteem depends not at all on the behaviour of others but rather upon acting in a manner which accords with God's plan for the world, and this may include the meek acceptance of humiliating treatment. On this view anger may emerge as a deadly sin in its own right, as an infringement of divine law.[10] But even on this view anger remains

---

[10]   Frank, ibid., makes this point.

linked to self-esteem, threatened here by the feeling of anger itself, and as a vice remains dependent on some form of pride regarded as sinful from the point of view of the meek and humble, but this is not to say that it is vicious in the sense under discussion. But whether anger may be righteous or not is in any case not to the point, for if righteous then it is not excessive. The best thing about the irascible, Aristotle thought, is that their anger stops quickly, for they do not repress but on the contrary vent it openly. So they rid themselves of their anger. And this indeed is the reason why aggressive anger does not share the precise viciousness of the other vices, for any self-harm that may arise from it is not precisely of their nature. In its active aggressiveness there is something open and within limits, even healthy, about anger, which is very much in contrast to the dispositions of the vicious. Anger seems unlikely to shrivel the soul or create a false self.

Wrath is not the only type of excessive anger Aristotle refers to: he also speaks of the 'bitter', of those who suppress their animosity and keep up their anger for a long time. They have to digest it internally and so labour under the weight of resentment. In Dante's *Inferno* they are those who are sunk deeply into the slime, who are not openly aggressive, and who cannot get their words out clearly. Such resentful anger lacks precisely that characteristic which made aggressive anger an unlikely candidate for viciousness in its own right.

Contrasting resentment with aggressive anger is not meant to imply that the former is free of aggressive desires; the difference is merely in these being expressed or repressed. Aggression, in the form of retaliation, is characteristic of the thoughts and desires constitutive of either type. It is given a prominent place in relevant discussions. For Aquinas, for instance, it is the basis for the distinction between righteous and sinful anger, for, he says, revenge may be desired both well and ill, hence which type of anger is experienced depends on the mode and object of this desire. Anger, like pride, concerns the relation between self and other, so in righteous anger we have got the relation right, in sinful anger we err in our own favour. Retaliation is merited in the former and not in the latter.[11] Thomas Reid uses the notion

---

[11] *ST* 2a2ae q. 158 art. 2.

of retaliation to make a different point. Accepting a distinction made by Bishop Butler, he characterizes two types of anger, for which, he says, we do not have different names in common language.[12] The first is a blind, impulsive reaction to any kind of hurt, the second a 'deliberate' anger in response to a perceived injury from others. Animals can experience anger in the first but not in the second sense, for thinking in terms of injury implies a grasp of the notion of justice which animals do not possess. Reid somewhat confuses the issue in that his description of the second type as 'cool' and 'deliberate' suggests that detached reasoning is involved whenever we react in this way. But all that is needed is that the relevant view of the situation, or, if dispositional, the perspective on life, include thinking in terms of rights, dues, deserts, and so on, and this does not conflict with a wholly impulsive reaction on relevant occasions. The distinction Reid seems to have in mind is that between 'primitive' and 'sophisticated' anger, which parallels the one that applied to cases of envy. It is of course sophisticated anger only which is relevant to a discussion of the features which might make anger a vice.

Sophisticated anger implies self-consciousness on the part of the agent; she has a view of her own standing. This means that, as is suggested in Reid's account, the 'object' of anger will be more complex than that of primitive anger, and so will also be the reaction itself. If in primitive anger that which occasions it is any kind of hurt whatever, then the reaction may be that of simple-minded revenge: you have hurt me, so now I am hurting you. In sophisticated anger, however, where the assessment of the occasion is bound up with self-evaluation, the aggressive reaction will correspondingly be motivated by more than this simple desire for revenge. As Reid also suggests, anger is aggressive always with a view to defence. As a defensive aggression it is, in sophisticated anger, protective of the person's view of her own position. This is so whether or not it is expressed in open behaviour. If so expressed then the person concerned has at least attempted to assert herself and show the other to be wrong, and in thus relieving her feelings has at least declared her own position and so has taken a step towards re-establishing herself. Total success

---

[12] *Essays on the Active Powers of the Human Mind*, essay 3, sect. 4: 'Of Malevolent Affection'. Bishop Butler, *Sermons*, sermon 8.

will depend on the reaction of the person addressed, and will depend, therefore, on her having succeeded in impressing on the other that he has not given her her due, that he has undervalued her and has not properly recognized her importance. The defensive aggression, aimed at righting an unmerited slur, will include the desire for such recognition.[13] Even if she keeps her thoughts and desires to herself they serve to protect her self-image, for they imply rejection of the view of herself which she believes to be expressed by the other. But if she keeps them to herself she will have failed to defend herself against the other, and thereby have failed even to attempt to achieve an acceptable acknowledgement of her worth.

There are, of course, many variations in the (sophisticated) anger-reaction; the threat to the image one wants others to recognize may range from the very slight to the extremely damaging, and the reaction to it will be more or less violent. A person may also, by identifying with certain groups of others, feel anger on their behalf, for any failure to recognize their importance will include herself among the victims. We may also be angry with ourselves, being frustrated by some inability to live up to our picture of ourselves. But both these reactions, whether towards others or ourselves, rely on a given self-image to be defended. This may be so even in the case where the anger-reaction is brought about by an inanimate object or impersonal event: the car will not start, the red light does not change. Often, no doubt, to feel anger on such occasions is merely a primitive reaction to frustrating circumstances. But it may also be an expression of outrage that one's wishes and expectations should not be given their due weight, and that consequently one's importance in the universe is not recognized, a realization which is particularly irritating in this context where desires for retaliation are without a suitable focus, so that one has to be found or manufactured. All these cases have as a common core the angry person's view that her rights (dues, deserts, claims, expectations) have not been taken as seriously as they ought to have been taken, and that consequently she herself has not been taken as seriously as she deserves to be taken. The consequent aggressive desires have two aspects: they

---

[13] Cf. Francis Fukuyama, *The End of History and the Last Man* (Harmondsworth: Penguin, 1992), ch. 15.

are partly revengeful, in retaliation for the undeserved neglect or misjudgement on the part of others. But partly they are also reformatory in the desire to get the other to recognize his error and to acknowledge her true worth. Anger is openly aggressive where such desires are expressed in action; it is resentful when they find no outlet.

The suggestion was that openly aggressive anger is a deadly vice only if based on vicious pride, but that resentful anger is in its own right a more promising candidate for the category of 'deadly vice'.[14] The reason is that although the dispositionally resentful feel themselves to be constantly undervalued, they keep this feeling to themselves, and the desires for retaliation and reparation are frustrated. But this does not make them go away. On the contrary, the feeling of being undervalued is allowed to fester. Finding no outlet, such feelings as well as the consequent feelings of hostility towards others will tend to grow, until they become uncontrollable. Shylock, deeply resenting Antonio who despises him because he is a Jew and a usurer, resolves to 'feed fat the ancient grudge I bear him'[15] until Antonio's inability to repay his debt offers him the chance to take revenge in the form of demanding a pound of flesh, a demand which in its enormity reflects the degree of accumulated hostility that has been nourished for a long time. The difference in resentment between inner state and outward behaviour is nicely illustrated by the whisperings of Mr Pugh, taking up morning tea to Mrs Pugh:[16]

> 'here's your arsenic, dear.
> And your weedkiller biscuit.
> I've throttled your parakeet.
> I've spat in the vases.
> I've put cheese in the mouseholes.
> Here's your . . .
> [*Door creaks open*
> . . . nice tea, dear.'

[14] One objection here may be that resentment is too closely connected with envy to qualify as a vice on its own. But while vicious envy involves resentment, the resentful need not necessarily be envious.

[15] *Merchant of Venice* I. iii. 41.   [16] Dylan Thomas, *Under Milkwood*.

On another occasion, when reprimanded on his table-manners, Mr Pugh, in the laboratory of his wishes, mixes especially for Mrs Pugh a venomous porridge unknown to toxicologists. His desire to impress his power on her, and his revenge for her treatment of him, are strongly felt but futile wishes, which can find an outlet only in imagination. So there is no attempt to alter the situation. Consequently, feelings of frustration cannot be relieved, but being left and renewed will become ever more deeply rooted and will tend to intensify the resentful's feelings of hostility towards those who refuse to give him his due.

The persistence of such feelings of frustration is bound to have a further negative effect, for in nourishing rather than venting his anger the agent is aware of having failed to assert himself; he has failed to take control and impress on others his true worth. He is weak and will suffer from feelings of impotence. The awareness of failing to make a stand will adversely affect his self-evaluation; he cannot be so admirable if he is defective in agency. His self-esteem, already perceived as under attack, is further shaken by this awareness, and the lurking thought that his deserts are perhaps not as great as he assumed may again increase his hostility towards those who refuse to give him that assurance which he so badly needs to restore his sense of his own worth.

The person wholly given to resentment will have characteristics which are sufficiently similar in structure to those in the grip of other vices to allow resentment to be regarded as being among the deadly ones. The person concerned need not be particularly vain, conceited, or arrogant for resentment to be corruptive, and so, unlike the more 'healthy' type of anger, its viciousness is not dependent on another, more basic, one. All that is required is that she feel unappreciated and overlooked, possibly initially on perfectly reasonable grounds. But however based, once resentment has taken root her perspective on life will include the expectation to be undervalued, and approaching others with this expectation in mind she tends to perceive it as being met. This attitude is in direct contrast to that of those prone to feel indignation. The indignant expect the other to give them their due, and any failure to do so on the other's part naturally puts her, the other, in the wrong. Treatment which is in their view not 'fitting' to their station is not seen by them as a threat

to their self-esteem but as some defect in the other. Indignation is
for this reason a more detached feeling than is resentment, and is
therefore sometimes thought to be felt only on behalf of others.
P. F. Strawson, for instance, speaks of indignation as 'the vicarious
analogue of resentment . . . resentment on behalf of another, where
one's own interests and dignity are not involved'.[17] But one can feel
indignation on one's own behalf, though since the situation is not
seen as affecting one's self-evaluation it is detachable, so to speak,
as resentment is not. The expectation to be undervalued indicates
some insecurity in one's position, and lacks the certainty, or possibly
complacency, of the indignant.

The resentful expect to be undervalued and tend to find their
expectations confirmed. Hence their resentment will become ever
more firmly established. Since they leave it unexpressed, they do not
offer others the opportunity to reason them out of this view, though
of course the more deeply caught in resentment the less is reasoning
likely to make an impression anyway. They seem to be caught in a
dilemma. In not venting their feelings they fail to assert themselves,
and non-assertiveness is deeply unflattering to self-esteem. But airing
their feelings would publicly disclose a weakness: they would admit
to the world that they cannot make their presence felt, for if they
could they would not be so constantly undervalued; and they would
further reveal the degree to which their self-esteem depends on
the evaluation of others. Such revelations would give others further
grounds for contempt, while the apparent impossibility of changing
their position for the better will further add to the resentfuls' feelings
of impotence. Their self-esteem, never very secure, will suffer further.
So they will nourish both an unsatisfactory view of themselves and, in
an attempt to protect their self-esteem, a hostile one towards others.
Like other deadly vices, resentment is thus self-nourishing and self-
frustrating: the agents' desire to be properly valued by others and
consequently by themselves cannot be fulfilled through the means
which they adopt. As in other deadly vices, there is confusion in their
evaluations, for they wish to impress their own worth on others, but

---

[17] 'Freedom and Resentment', *Freedom and Resentment and Other Essays* (New
York: Methuen, 1980), 14.

are not themselves sufficiently convinced of that worth to have the courage to take the relevant steps. A disclosure of their feelings may after all reveal the world's assessment of them to be correct. Painful and frustrating though their position may be, keeping their feelings to themselves is still seen as a form of self-protection.

6 INTERCONNECTIONS

I

Given the structural similarities between the various vices because of which they were chosen as a set in the first place, it is not surprising that there should be overlaps between them, or that those in the grip of one of these vices should also naturally be exposed to another. A clear case is the relation between resentment and envy. The resentful and the envious share feelings of impotence and of hostility towards others. These are miserable feelings, and suffering them will reinforce both their sense of failure and their vengeful attitude towards the world. Deep-rooted attitudes are not only difficult to shed; they also tend to prevent the agent from realizing that it might be desirable for them to be shed, and a fostering of their sense of grievance is a familiar feature of both the resentful and the envious. A distinction between them is that these feelings are differently focused, for resentment is not, like envy, crucially linked to a comparison with others. Their aims, too, it seems, are somewhat different: the envious desire an esteem-worthy self, the resentful recognition as an esteem-worthy self. But it is hardly possible to keep these aims apart. The resentfuls' self-esteem is dependent on recognition by others; if this were not so their resentment would not be so all-consuming. It would leave room for feelings of indignation in that they would be convinced that their worth, so plain to themselves, ought to be accepted everywhere. And for the envious it is at least natural that their hoped-for view of themselves as esteem-worthy should require the thought that this is also how they would be and want to be seen by others. The envious resent those they perceive as better off, and the resentful may quite naturally feel envy of those to whom esteem is accorded and who thus are in a position to value themselves. Together envy and resentment are the main ingredients of the state, or process, labelled 'ressentiment', according to Nietzsche the morality of slaves.[1] It is a 'slavish' state in its lack of assertiveness, in the person's failure to do anything about his position which he conceives of as being ignored or despised by the in—this respect—better off. All he can do to relieve his feelings is to indulge in imaginary revenge, feelings which either he will be unable to express, or, if he does find an outlet, are inappropriately directed.

Similar connections have already been mentioned: the miserly naturally are also covetous in tending to wish continually to increase their hoard, and so are the envious, in wanting that which belongs to another. Their respective desires indicate two dimensions of covetousness: the intensity of the desire for more and more, and the (possibly consequent) desire for another's property. Aquinas defines 'covetousness' as 'the immoderate love of possession'. It can be thought of, he says, as either a sin against one's neighbour, if one wants to keep more than one has a right to possess; or as a sin against oneself, since a man's inordinate love of possession 'causes disorder in his affections'.[2] Aquinas thinks in terms of external riches only, such as the miser's golden ducats. But covetousness need not be so restricted. The vain, for instance, may be said to be covetous in their desire for flattery. Thought of as a 'sin against oneself' covetousness is indeed a feature shared by the vicious, the only exception being sloth, where disengagement prohibits the experience of any kind of deeply rooted desire. The avaricious, envious, proud, and resentful can all be said to be inordinate in their desire to have a certain position for themselves secured or (in the case of the arrogant) maintained, excessive in that it is too intense in its concentration on that object, and, since it cannot be satisfied, excessive also in the need for its constant renewal.

Covetousness would appear quite obviously to be a prominent component of the remaining two vices, lust and gluttony, and thus be that which links these to the others and makes them members of the same set. In other ways, however, the lustful and the glutton seem to

---

[1] *On the Genealogy of morals*, pt. I. See also Max Scheler, *Ressentiment* (New York: Free Press, 1961).

[2] *Summa Theologiae* (*ST*) 2a2ae q. 118, art. 1.

be in a class apart: they seem engaged in the search for pleasure as the others are not. Where these were seen to try to protect and guard, the glutton and the lustful seem active in the pursuit of something more positive. Traditionally lust and gluttony were classed together as both concerning bodily pleasures, and it may be that their inclusion in the list of mortal sins was simply on the grounds that indulgence in such pleasures at the expense of the spiritual is against the order of reason. Lust, Aquinas thinks, causes havoc in a man's mind, and gluttony, by deifying the pleasures of food and drink, turns his mind away from the love of God. Hence in both cases man is subject to inordinate desires and acts against reason, and 'the virtues of the soul are destroyed by them' (*ST* 2a2ae qq. 148 and 153) It remains to be seen whether this destruction resembles the corruption of the self found in the other vices.

If lust and gluttony are both concerned with bodily pleasures then the only difference between them would be in the kind of pleasure they seek, namely those of sex and food respectively. Further differences follow: lust involves others, and the relevant attitude towards these may well be crucial to its being classed as a vice. Gluttony, on the other hand, does not essentially involve others, and to be excessively fond of eating and drinking, or of eating and drinking well, while not particularly admirable and presumably full of health hazards, seems a relatively harmless state. It appears to be the simpler of the two, and I shall consider it first.

According to Aquinas, the glutton's case can be summed up by saying that he exceeds in what he eats, or in how much, how, or when he eats. He wants too much sumptuous food daintily prepared, and he will eat too often or eat greedily. In these various ways his desire for food (and drink) is 'inordinate' or excessive.[3] Food, then, is his consuming interest, and something will have to be said about the glutton's specific object of desire. But gluttony is also said to be concerned with the pleasures of the palate, and this implies that it is

---

[3] Aquinas includes drinking under the heading of 'gluttony' though he discusses drunkenness separately. The points here made in relation to excess eating apply equally to excess drinking. Aquinas seems to think that every glutton is a gourmet, for he wants to see his food daintily prepared. But a glutton need not be so refined and fastidious in his tastes.

the pleasure of eating rather than the food itself for which the glutton has an inordinate desire. From this point of view the glutton is simply a pleasure-seeker. So one way of approaching what may be the vice of the glutton is to look at the nature of the pleasure he appears to be after. Eating, like drinking and sex, is commonly thought to be a pleasure. This is not to say, of course, that everyone will take pleasure in such pleasures, but it is to say that it is quite normal to do so, that pleasures are there to be enjoyed, and that consequently their enjoyment is wholly understandable and does not require further explanation. In this respect the glutton differs from, for instance, the miser, whose desires and behaviour were far from self-explanatory. The pleasure of eating is primarily a pleasure of sensation in that it has a large sensory component. In this it differs from other types of pleasure, such as that derived from reading a book or digging the garden, in which sensations need not play any part at all. Sometimes the distinction between these has been described as one between 'passive' and 'active' pleasure, where the latter is 'the pleasure which a man derives from doing things which he is *keen on doing, enjoys* doing, or *likes* to do.[4] At first sight this labelling may confuse rather than clarify, for eating after all is an activity which the glutton likes to engage in. But if it is the pleasure of eating he enjoys rather than the activity then the puzzle will disappear: the pleasure he finds in eating is in the sensations of taste he experiences, and these are occurrences, not activities. His pleasure is the reaction to sensations of taste such as sweetness or juiciness. It is sensations of this type as the source of unique and exquisite pleasure which Balzac's gourmet Pons seeks in his periods of gastric nostalgia: 'Pons yearned for certain kinds of *crème*, each one a poem; for certain white sauces, every one a masterpiece; for certain dishes of truffled poultry, all ravishing to the taste; and above all for those Rhenish carp which are only found in Paris' (*Cousin Pons*, ch. 7). For a gourmet such as Cousin Pons the sensations of taste enjoyed are likely to be complex and varied; possibly it is the precise combination of, say, the tartness of the sauce and its creamy softness which is needed for undiluted pleasure.

---

[4] G. H. von Wright, *The Varieties of Goodness*, (London: Routledge and Kegan Paul, 1953), ch. 4, 64–5. Italics in the text.

But no degree of complexity or refinement alters their essential nature. Sensations, unlike emotions and moods, have no intentional content, and so lack an 'internal' as well as an 'external' object. That is to say, sensations lack not only a focus, but lack also that cognitive element which is expressed in propositions stating how the person concerned views a particular situation or the world in general. Moods and emotions contain a reference to some object of thought (the situation, the world), sensations do not. Sensations, then, are both passive and non-intentional. Indeed, their non-intentionality indicates a further dimension of their passivity: sensations are passive not merely because they are occurrences as opposed to activities; they are passive precisely because they have no cognitive content. Without a reference beyond themselves to some aspect of the world they lack that which, in the case of emotions and even moods, makes it possible to at any rate try and exercise some control over them. No view of the world being involved, there is no way of altering the view of the world. Sensation-based pleasures share the properties of sensations; they occur only if and while the relevant sensations are experienced, they have no life of their own. In particular, like sensations they are non-intentional, their content is sensuous and not cognitive. Consequently, pleasures of sensation are altogether outside the province of the will.[5]

Pleasures of the palate are such pleasures of sensation. It may not be entirely accurate to think of the glutton as seeking simply these kinds of pleasure. As Scruton points out, while the pleasures of taste, touch, and smell always have a large sensory component, those of the eye and ear tend to be intentional pleasures,[6] and it is at least possible that the glutton also experiences some pleasure of the eye, an aesthetic pleasure, perhaps, in the arrangement and colouring of the food.[7] However, his enjoyment of pleasures of the palate is seen as his distinctive mark, so this is what the glutton is taken to pursue.

---

[5] The distinction between intentional and non-intentional pleasures is drawn by Roger Scruton, *Sexual Desire*, (London: Weidenfeld and Nicolson, 1986), 18–19.

[6] Ibid. 246.

[7] Aesthetic pleasures are the mark of the gourmet, and the more such pleasures dominate over wholly sensory ones the less is a gourmet likely to share fully the characteristics here ascribed to the sensory pleasure-seeking glutton.

They are that which his activities aim at, and are not merely the by-product of some other pursuit, such as eating to keep healthy. If this is the glutton's overall aim then it is not hard to see why he should be thought to devote himself to the wrong end by all those who have 'proper' human ends in mind, or have views, at any rate, about the direction a human life should take. This applies not merely to those who, like Aquinas, think that the glutton sins in irrationally replacing the love of God by the love of pleasure. Kant, too, thinks the glutton irrational and in breach of a duty to himself. He does not develop his talents, and so does not act as a rational being would but instead indulges in a contemptible 'beastly' vice.[8] Similarly, in Mill's view, someone pursuing merely pleasures of sensation would devote himself entirely to the 'lower' pleasures, those which non-human animals can also experience, and hence would neglect his higher faculties and thus offend human dignity. He would be unable to achieve the type of happiness which alone can satisfy those beings who are capable of experiencing the 'higher' pleasures.[9]

There is a point in these complaints which can be extracted without commitment to any of the diverse frameworks offered by Aquinas, Kant, and Mill. On the present picture of the glutton his overall aim is to achieve a passive, non-intentional state of consciousness. Such states are in their very nature relatively short-lived, so that the given aim requires constant renewal of the search. Moreover, the nature of the aim implies a state of isolation. This is so because in its non-intentionality the relevant states of consciousness do not reach beyond themselves, they do not connect with the world or with each other, and so cannot generate further, more outgoing desires and interests. Bradley, in his attack on Hedonism,[10] refers to states of pleasures of sensation as 'self-feeling', to bring out the point that they are no more than personal feeling-states and hence wholly subjective; they exist only as long as the subject feels them; they have no reference beyond this and no reality behind them. At best, then, the glutton's self is a severely impoverished one. There is no room

---

[8] Immanuel Kant, lecture, 'Duties towards the Body Itself', *Lectures on Ethics*.

[9] John Stuart Mill, *Utilitarianism*, ch. 2.

[10] *Ethical Studies* (London: Oxford University Press, 1962), essay 3, 'Pleasure for Pleasure's Sake'.

for development. He may of course look for more and different sorts of food to see whether his pleasure can be enhanced. But if this is to be seen as development at all then it is a poor one since it moves in one direction only and lacks the dimensions and complexities open to human beings. If the glutton is someone who pursues nothing but the pleasures of the palate then he has dissociated himself from the world to such an extent that his self will lack all substance. In this respect he resembles the arrogantly proud: like the proud, he is totally enclosed in himself, imprisoned in his own subjectivity. Both are wholly intent on reflexive ends, though on different levels, for unlike the proud the glutton need not think of himself or his aims as being superior in any way. Not surprisingly, this makes him a much less complex character, for the desire for pleasure raises fewer problems than does the desire for a unique position. The glutton, like the proud, cannot properly think in terms of values at all, for these require a degree of objectivity which is lacking in his case. But since he does not have to think of himself as having special and superior values, this inability does not raise the kind of problems which related to pride. However, while the glutton escapes from these, he remains below the level where reasoned evaluating has its place, and so it can be said of him, as it could be said of the slothful, that he does not engage in practical reasoning at all, and consequently lacks a vital feature of human agency.

The glutton as a pleasure-seeker may, then, indeed be seen as a corrupter of self. If 'pleasure-seeker' exhausts the characterization then he is a hedonist whose pleasures of sensation, as it happens, are those of the palate. But a characterization wholly in terms of sensations makes it appear that the source of these sensations, food and drink, is quite incidental to the glutton's situation, and this must be wrong. To qualify as a glutton it is essential that his pleasures be derived from food. So there is another point of view from which, possibly, gluttony may emerge as a vice, namely that the glutton's interest in food and the value he attaches to it are such that other objects of interest and value are by him seen as negligible. Something has gone wrong with his relation to food, and to explain it by reference to an addiction to the pleasures of the palate does not seem sufficient, for it leaves unanswered the question of why he is so addicted to this particular pleasure that it leaves no room in his life for anything else.

While enjoyment of pleasures of sensation is quite understandable, such excess of it is not.

Food, obviously, is nourishment, and an interest in food can be taken to be (among other things) an interest in nourishment. The glutton may be quite aware—if he gives a thought to the matter—that for physical health and energy the quantity or quality of the desired food is not required. Nevertheless, he feels he has a need for it. So it seems that, unlike the proud, the glutton does not feel himself to be self-sufficient; on the contrary, in his view his self needs to be nourished. If he has such a need then he feels himself to be undernourished and hence deficient in some respect. His self is not an altogether healthy self. But what, precisely, is lacking? Gluttony, together with lust but as opposed to, for example, pride, was classed as a sin of the flesh rather than the spirit. Sins of the flesh, though still mortal, were thought to be less culpable than sins of the spirit.[11] They may be seen, perhaps, as being more 'warm-hearted' sins, in that eating and drinking may encourage social intercourse;[12] and the glutton is not as coldly disdainful a character as is the proud. He is after all capable of experiencing the positive feeling of pleasure, and that in itself makes his defects more human than are those of the other vicious. The need for nourishment adds a further dimension to the glutton in that he cannot now be seen as being merely in search of pleasures of sensation. He may still be a pleasure-seeker, but the pleasures he wants are meant to nourish. No doubt he looks on nourishment as something to be savoured and enjoyed, but not as merely yielding a pleasure which will live and die with the sensations of the palate. Nourishment lasts longer than do the pleasures of eating. What he wants is some more long-lasting pleasure or comfort, a health-giving and heart-warming pleasure. If this is what he needs then this is what he lacks.

In literature indications of gluttony are found among those who feel themselves in need of warmth in the form of human affection.

---

[11] Aquinas, *ST* 2a2ae q. 148 art. 3. Dante places the gluttonous and the lustful in the upper purgatory, closest to the earthly paradise.

[12] Kant ('Duties towards the Body Itself') rather surprisingly thinks that drink in particular tends to promote sociability and conversation, and that this is some excuse for it.

One such character was Cousin Pons, who thought himself unlovable. Another case is Mrs Clenham in Dickens's *Little Dorrit*. Mrs Clenham leads a solitary life. She has little human contact and never leaves her room. She thinks of herself as being imprisoned and in bonds (ch. 5), and is described as 'a lady without pity, without love, cold as a stone' (ch. 30). There is no emotional warmth in her life, and she is capable of neither giving nor receiving affection. Curiously, at first sight, this cold woman is a gourmet. Her food, which is very different from that eaten in the kitchen, is brought to her on a tray, and the preparation and consumption are something of a ritual. In the evenings she is served with a dish of little rusks 'and a small precise pat of butter, cool, symmetrical, white and plump'. Some of the rusks are to be buttered, others dipped into a hot drink of port-wine, lemon, and spice, an 'odorous mixture, measured out and compounded with as much nicety as a physician's prescription'. Mid-mornings she is served with oysters, 'eight in number, circularly set out on a white plate with a white napkin, flanked by a slice of buttered French roll, and a little compact glass of cool wine and water' (chs. 3 and 4). These exquisite little dishes are in odd contrast to the general bleakness which otherwise surrounds Mrs Clenham. But her desire for particular types of food served in a particular manner is not incongruous when it is connected with her dim awareness of something lacking, of some hunger she wants to still.

It is perhaps possible to see signs of a similar hunger in the controversial character of Shakespeare's 'surfeit-swelled' Sir John Falstaff, whose natural habitat appears to have been the Boar's Head Tavern. At a time when the Prince's rejection of him is still far in the future, he replies to Hal's question: 'Sirrah, do I owe you a thousand pounds?' with: 'A thousand pound, Hal! A million. Thy love is worth a million: thou owest me thy love' (Henry IV, I. iii. 3). The question was ironic, the reply seems serious. So maybe even at this stage Falstaff is far from certain of Hal's friendship, and is looking for something more nourishing than mere pleasures of sensation. But perhaps his reply should not be taken that seriously, since at present Falstaff appears to be quite happy and at ease. If so, he may be thought to remain on the hedonistic level and not in need of more substantial nourishment. He is not worried about the state of the self because he himself is among the many things he refuses to take seriously. It is true that he needs Hal's affection, but while he believes himself to be assured of that he can afford to enjoy not only satisfying his appetites, but enjoy also the spectacle of his enjoyment of these pleasures.[13] He can distance himself from himself, a relatively self-saving device which, among all the vicious, is open perhaps to the hedonistic glutton alone. At least his superficial, solely pleasure-loving self will be free from the torture of underlying self-doubt.

For the Mrs Clenham type of glutton, however, oysters, lemon, and port are hardly the right answer. She wants a, in some respects, healthier self. But this cannot be achieved by the means she adopts. She looks in the wrong direction, for it is not food in its literal sense she needs. All this can yield are short-lived sensuous states of consciousness, so that she nourishes herself in the most superficial way there is. Pleasures of sensation are too fleeting and rootless to constitute by themselves a satisfactory diet. Just as food and drink are poor substitutes for the type of nourishment she really needs, so pleasures of the palate are not those she really seeks. It is not surprising, therefore, that this glutton has to continue her search, and that her desires are insatiable.

Lust is linked with gluttony in that both are concerned with pleasures of the flesh. In some respects lust may even be seen as a case of gluttony, for the lustful appear to view the object of their desire as something to be consumed, sometimes quite obviously so. A very clear illustration can be found in a recent discussion of the presentation of women in the novels of Charles Dickens.[14] In these novels very young, marriageable girls tend to be presented as visually slight and delicate; they are passive and innocent. But they also appeal to the palate: Ruth Pinch, for instance, preparing a steak pie, 'burst out heartily into such a charming little laugh of triumph, that the pudding need have no other seasoning to commend it to the taste of

---

[13] A view taken by A. C. Bradley, 'The Rejection of Falstaff', in *Oxford Lectures on Poetry*, reprinted in G. K. Hunter (ed.), *King Henry IV Parts 1 and 2*, Casebook Studies (London: Macmillan, 1970).

[14] Patricia Ingham, *Dickens, Women and Language* (Toronto: University of Toronto Press, 1992), ch. 2, 'Nubile Girls'. The examples used in the text are taken from that chapter.

any reasonable man on earth', and for chops and potatoes she is seen as the best sauce ever invented (*Martin Chuzzlewit*, chs. 39 and 37). Similarly, David Copperfield, at the first meeting with his future wife Dora, was of the impression that he 'dined off Dora, entirely' (ch. 26). Ruth and Dora are here seen in terms of delicious food capable of providing sensuous pleasure as well as nourishment. They are seen lustfully, the lust being expressed in gluttonous terms. The other thus appears as the source of certain sensations, a sex-object appealing to the palate. If this is the only appeal then the lustful closely resembles the hedonistic glutton. But he may quite naturally also see the woman concerned as a provider of nourishing food. Either way, the points already made about the glutton would equally apply to him.

The parallel between lust and gluttony is, however, not as close as this account suggests. This is so because the pleasure sought by the lustful tends to be more complex than is that pursued by the glutton. Roger Scruton defines lust as a 'genuine sexual desire, from which the goal of erotic love has been excluded, and in which whatever tends towards that goal—tenderness, intimacy, fidelity, dependence—is curtailed or obstructed'.[15] Given that definition, a clarification of the concept of lust must clearly begin with some account of sexual desire. As is often pointed out, this cannot be a desire merely for sexual pleasure, if that is thought to be no more than a pleasure of sensation, for such a view cannot explain how it is that another being can be an essential component in the project of desire.[16] Sexual desire includes desire for union with some particular other, and the desire for some response. If, therefore, pleasure is thought to be the overall aim of sexual desire, then it is a more complex pleasure in that it includes an intentional component. This is complex in itself. Since it is the pleasure derived from the fulfilment of sexual desire its complexity hinges on that of the desire.

---

[15] Scruton, *Sexual Desire*, 344.

[16] E.g. ibid. ch. 4; Jean-Paul Sartre, *Being and Nothingness*, tr. Hazel E. Barnes (London: Methuen, 1981), pt. 3, ch. 3; Thomas Nagel, 'Sexual Perversion', in *Mortal Questions* (Cambridge: Cambridge University Press, 1979); Max Scheler, *The Nature of Sympathy*, tr. Peter Heath (London: Routledge and Kegan Paul, 1979). Freud refers to the complexity of the sexual aim when he speaks of the 'overvaluation' of its object which 'spreads over into the psychological sphere'; *Three Essays on the Theory of Sexuality*. I.

Sexual desire is variously described by Nagel and Scruton, though based by both on Sartre's highly complicated and rather obscure account. Nagel speaks of the paradigm case of mutual desire as involving a system of superimposed mutual perceptions, not only of the sexual object but also of oneself. There is a reflexive mutual recognition. Sex 'involves a desire that one's partner be aroused by the recognition of one's desire that he or she be aroused'.[17] This makes the point that sexual desire aims at reciprocity, which in turn means that a particular other is essentially involved. In Scruton's interpretation of Sartre's view, this desire aims at the other's 'incarnation': a summoning of the other's consciousness into the other's flesh so that there it can be possessed'.[18]

These characterizations make it clear that in sexual desire the other is not regarded as merely an object which, like delicious food, can give rise to pleasurable sensations. The involvement of the other's consciousness is essential, and essential, therefore, also to the consequent pleasure. If, then, as Scruton suggests, the lustful have genuine sexual desires, then they cannot be accused of treating the other as merely an object of their appetite. On the other hand, the other-consciousness they seek is of a limited nature, for they do not desire reciprocity of intimacy or tenderness or commitment. For the satisfaction of their pleasure it is enough that the other is aroused by recognition of their desire that they be aroused. This means that although an individual other person is necessarily involved, this other is not perceived by the lustful as being particularly individualized; their perspectives and general emotional reactions are irrelevant. Consequently there are these two sides to the lustful: his attention will be wholly concentrated on the individual partner, for it is *her* desire he wants to arouse. Hence he charms and seduces. But since his aim is so narrow his interest in her will flag once it is achieved, and again, since his aim is so narrow there is no question of developing any form of personal relationship. Hence the lustful are naturally promiscuous.

This account of the lustful excludes from the set those who may simply desire another's body and may not be particularly concerned

---

[17] Nagel, *Mortal Questions*, 47.   [18] Scruton, *Sexual Desire*, 121.

to elicit a response. If they are to be included then their sexual desires may be thought to be perverted, or anyway to be of a cruder kind than is here assumed. But this complication in the identification of possible candidates for lust can be ignored in the present context. If it is sexual pleasure they are after, then they will resemble in relevant respects the hedonist already discussed. If it is physical conquest only they have in mind, then whatever reasons there may be for thinking lust of the complex type a deadly vice will apply to the cruder one as well.

Don Juan may be taken to be a paradigm case of the lustful, in particular that version of the Don which is presented in Mozart's opera *Don Giovanni*. The dimensions of his promiscuity are fully illustrated by the entries in the list which his servant Leporello keeps of 'the beauties my master has loved'. There are not only unbelievably many of these (notoriously 1,003 in Spain alone), they are also of every conceivable kind:

> Among these are peasant girls,
> Maidservants, city girls,
> Countesses, baronesses,
> Marchionesses, princesses,
> Women of every rank,
> Every shape, every age. . . .
> He seduces the old ones
> For the pleasure of adding to the list. . . .

The Don is not choosy: any woman is a potential name to be added to the list, and which one in fact appears seems to be arbitrary. W. H. Auden suggests that this sort of attitude is not that of a sensual libertine. That type is represented by, for example, the Duke in Verdi's *Rigoletto*, who would not dream of looking twice at a woman who is old or plain. The Don's pleasure in seducing women, Auden thinks, 'is not sensual but arithmetical; his satisfaction lies in adding one more name to his list . . . he might just as well have chosen to collect stamps.'[19] But the Don does not collect stamps, and although it is true that he takes pleasure in adding to the list, that pleasure must have a more solid foundation than simply seeing a lengthening string of names; he does not, after all, ever bother

---

[19] 'Balaam and his Ass', in *The Dyer's Hand and Other Essays*.

to look at the list. It may be that the Duke and the Don are two rather different instances of the same type. The latter does not discriminate because, as Kierkegaard puts it, 'he desires in every woman the whole of womanhood, and therein lies the sensuously idealising power with which he at once embellishes and overcomes his prey'. His sensuously idealizing explains his lack of discrimination: 'He rejuvenates the older woman into the beautiful middle age of womanhood; he matures the child almost instantly.'[20]

'Desiring in every woman the whole of womanhood' encapsulates the two aspects of the lustful: the particular partner of the moment deserves full attention since she represents all womanhood. But since she represents all womanhood any other representative will do as well, so there can be no reason for fidelity. The differentiation between women, if any, is of the slightest, for it can be a variation only of a feature shared by all, and so it must remain on the level of the sensual. Although, then, while the other is not regarded as merely an object, she (or he) is not seen as an individual person, either. This gives some support to the Kantian view that the lustful merely use their partners, and will cast them aside 'as one casts away a lemon which has been sucked dry'.[21] It remains unclear, however, precisely what in this state of affairs is so attractive to the lustful themselves that they let pursuit of representatives of womanhood (or manhood) dominate their lives.

On Scruton's interpretation of Sartre's view the aim of sexual desire was to summon the other's consciousness into her flesh, so as to be able to possess her there. The other's consciousness is made incarnate so that it can be possessed. Possession and conquest are crucial components of the desire, and the pleasure derived from its fulfilment is to a considerable extent the pleasure of having conquered. The point of Leporello's list is to record such conquests, which, since 'consciousness has been summoned', cannot be seen as

---

[20] 'The Immediate Stages of the Erotic or the Musical Erotic', *Either/Or*, i. (The Duke, a not very interesting character, may simply lack the imagination and 'idealising power' which the Don possesses.)

[21] 'Duties towards the Body in Respect of Sexual Impulse', *Lectures on Ethics*. For Kant it is of course the emphasis on sensuality which is so deplorable. As far as individualization is concerned, the rational being is no better off than is the object of the lustful.

being merely physical. Sartre (speaking of the lover rather than the lustful) points out that if his desire were for mere physical conquest it would be more easily satisfied than in fact it is. He illustrates this point by reference to Proust: his protagonist Marcel 'who instals his mistress in his home, who can see her and possess her at any hour of the day ... ought to be free from worry. Yet we know that he is, on the contrary, continually gnawed by anxiety.' This is so, Sartre thinks, because what Marcel wants to possess is Albertine's consciousness, her perspective on life and on him in particular. But 'through her consciousness Albertine escapes Marcel even when he is at her side'.[22] So, Sartre concludes, it is certain that the lover wishes to capture a consciousness.

Sartre's conclusion seems rather rashly drawn since Marcel's love is so obsessive and neurotic that it can hardly be thought of as a norm. He wants to catch every thought that passes through Albertine's mind. In particular, he wants to be assured that Albertine loves him, loves only him, and that her love is given freely. As Sartre puts it: 'it is the Other's freedom that we want to get hold of',[23] that is, the lover wants the other's response to be freely given and not mechanically produced. This seems a 'normal' desire which need not be neurotically distorted by constant suspicion and hence constant need for reassurance, both components of Marcel's attitude. It is a desire of the lustful as well as of the lover, for his seduction would hardly be a conquest if the other's response to it were due to, and known to be due to, some love-potion which produced an automatic response. But it is all the lustful require, for it is enough for the conquest of a representative of womanhood. While the consciousness Marcel desired to possess was excessively rich, that wanted by the lustful is at the other end of the scale, and is extremely meagre, consisting of no more than a response due to the recognition of being desired to so respond.

The object and nature of the lustful's desires are such that they can be seen to resemble in crucial respects those of other vicious

---

[22] Sartre, *Being and Nothingness*, 366.

[23] From this arises Sartre's 'paradox of desire': necessarily aiming at something which cannot be attained. Scruton discusses the paradox, *Sexual Desire*, 94–5 and 120 ff.

characters. Don Giovanni, the suggested paradigm, was said to see particular women as merely representatives of womanhood. If so, then it seems that what he is aiming at is the conquest of all womanhood. This in turn means that the pleasure derived from conquest will be short-lived, for there is a lot of womanhood left and many more representatives to be conquered. As Kierkegaard points out, the Don is always in a hurry: as soon as he has succeeded (or failed) with one woman he looks for another. He has no time, or does not allow himself to have time, to feel anxious about possible failure. It is important, Kierkegaard also thinks, that the most memorable figure on Leporello's list, one thousand and three, is both odd and incidental, for it leaves the impression that the list is by no means closed, but that, on the contrary, the Don will hurry on as long as he lives. The same desire will repeat itself endlessly.

As a consequence, the desired possession of (limited) consciousness is so fleeting that it cannot but remain on the minimal level indicated, and so there is not even the possibility of further knowledge of the other, no chance of any kind of intimacy. The pleasure provided by this possession is wholly derived from the thought that the other's response is brought about by his desire that she so respond, and this is a boost to him, a confirmation of his power. But since the desire is constantly renewed, it cannot be a boost that has lasting effect. Whatever the (non-neurotic) lover wishes to possess in possessing consciousness, it is a good which is at least capable of developing into something enriching and significant. By contrast, the lustful's relationships are not significant and cannot be enriching. They reflect a very meagre self, no more than that of the sexual conqueror. But even this identity is not secure, for that image of himself has to be constantly renewed. His search for confirmation as powerful is therefore doomed, and the lustful, like other vicious characters, turns out to have needs which are frustrated by his very attempts to meet them.

On this account of the lustful the difference between him and the hedonistic glutton is that the aim of the former but not that of the latter includes provoking another's response. But the two types seem to draw more closely together when the glutton is thought of as looking for more than hedonistic pleasures and is in search of nourishment, of warmth and affection. In that case the difference is in

the nature of the response desired, and consequently in the nature of
the hoped-for self-image; the powerful conqueror as opposed to the
nourished (warmed, loved) person. From this point of view gluttony,
in sharp contrast to lust, remains a 'warm-hearted' vice—a difference
between them which is ignored if both are regarded as being simply
'sins of the flesh'.

In their ever-frustrated and hence never-ending search for an
acceptable self the glutton and the lustful share the crucial features
of the envious, the avaricious, and the proud. It is their common
denominator. They are distinguished from one another by their
specific differences of aim, by the particular view they want to be
able to take of themselves and their position in the world. Only the
slothful do not conform to this pattern, for they have given up on
themselves. However, they, too, connect with other vices. As was
indicated earlier, they resemble the arrogantly proud in that neither
type faces the problem of acquiring a valued self, though of course
their manner of failing to do so is very different: while the one thinks
that the situation is so hopeless that no effort can be worthwhile, the
other assumes that he has already succeeded and any effort to acquire
worth therefore unnecessary. There is also a link between the busy
slothful and the hedonistic glutton, for both are in a position where
short-lived states of consciousness need constant renewal. And there
may be a further, more general connection between the slothful and
the other types of vicious: being prey to desires which are insatiable
they are all involved in a circle of repetitive striving, and repetition
breeds boredom. This is perhaps most likely to be so in the case
of the lustful where each conquest, the temporary fulfilment of the
desire, must be very much like another: 'Emma was like any other
mistress; and the charm of novelty gradually slipping away like a
garment, laid bare the eternal monotony of passion, whose forms
and phrases are forever the same' (Rodolph's view of his affair with
Emma Bovary).

The boredom here described attaches to the repeated experience
of ever the same sort of desire and consequent engagement in ever
the same sort of activity. But further, there is also the threat of

boredom and disengagement if the vicious concerned should realize that their aim is unattainable and their desires unfulfillable. Their *raison d'être* will disappear, and nothing will seem worth striving for. The indifference of sloth seems an ever-present threat from which they can escape only by maintaining their self-protective self-deception.

7 'CAPITAL VICES'

THE characterization of the vices as 'deadly' has been explained in terms of the fatal harm they bring to those who possess them. Little has as yet been said about their effect on others, though there have been indications that at least potentially they are likely to be harmful to others as well. Traditionally, the 'deadly sins' were thought to be also 'capital sins', on the grounds that their nature was such that it encouraged the emergence of other sins. A sin was then a capital one if it was the source, or potential source, of further sins, described as its 'daughters' or 'offspring'. Aquinas defines as 'capital' a vice that 'has a very desirable end, so that through desire for that end, a man proceeds to commit many sins, all of which are said to arise from that vice as from a principal vice' (*Summa Theologiae* (*ST*) 2a2ae q. 153 art. 4). This definition suggests that the deadly vices, if also capital, provide the agent with an end which is so attractive that he will adopt any means whatever to achieve it regardless of whether the means adopted are themselves vicious. Aquinas holds that an end is particularly desirable if it is seen as having as a constituent one of the conditions of happiness, 'which is desirable by its very nature' (q. 148 art. 5). Pleasure is one of these conditions, and hence the prospect of it may be so tempting that people may do anything for its sake. Lust and gluttony, being specifically concerned with pleasure, are therefore prominent among the capital sins, and Aquinas even hints that at any rate gluttony, though a deadly sin, is a danger to virtue not primarily because of this, but because of the vices which arise from it (q. 148 art. 2).

It is quite obvious, of course, that if an end is desired to such an extent that other considerations are negligible then many evil deeds may be committed in the course of pursuing it. A person may lie, rob, or murder for that end. If this is what Aquinas has in mind then being in the grip of a deadly vice may provide motivation for any immoral deed whatever. Maybe it does, but this is not quite the point, for the question at issue does not concern individual evil actions performed on this or that particular occasion. The question is rather whether the disposition of the vicious is such that possessing a particular vice they thereby have further vicious tendencies as well.

Aquinas considers this point as well. In his discussions of individual sins regarded as capital he thinks of dispositions rather than acts. Speaking of the daughters of lust, for instance, he picks out blindness of mind, lack of moderation, and lack of judgement. No doubt the lustful have such defects, but these can hardly be specifically linked to that particular vice. The common flaw of all the deadly sins, according to Aquinas, is that they interfere with the right order of reason and passion, and blindness of mind, lack of moderation, and lack of judgement seem merely specifications of this shared general flaw. All the vicious will as a matter of course suffer from these sorts of irrationality, so that we do not learn anything in particular about the lustful. In other discussions Aquinas does concentrate on the specific characteristics of the relevant vice. So, for example, when speaking of sloth he cites as its offspring idleness, uneasiness of mind, restlessness of body, and instability. But here the difficulty is that these could be seen to be different ways in which sloth itself might be manifested, rather than further vices for which the slothful state was responsible.

To think of the capital vices as the offspring of deadly vices seemed to suggest that these were separate vices, identifiable independently of the characterization of the deadly ones. But given Aquinas's account of the relevant dispositions this was perhaps a mistaken view. The relation of deadly to capital vice he mentions seemed too close for mutual independence. So perhaps the metaphor of the former 'being the source of' the latter should be differently interpreted. It may be that the dispositions of the vicious are such that built into their characterizations are vices harmful to others. In that case to speak of the deadly vices as capital is simply to change one's point of view, to shift from considering their harmful effect on the agent to thinking of their harmful or potentially harmful effect on others. So we could ask, following Aquinas's procedure: first, do the deadly vices collectively share features which are (potentially) harmful to others, and secondly, what, if any, are the features of individual vices which (potentially) are likely to harm others?

Harm in general is relative to some parameter or framework.[1] Applied to the self 'harm' was taken to mean 'corruption of the self and the consequent impossibility of leading a flourishing life, sometimes of leading a life at all'. Such a notion of harm is, as Wiggins puts it, 'not innocent of the metaphysics of personhood' (p. 11). A person was thought of as an active being, capable of evaluating her desires and having an interest in leading what would be from her point of view a good life, so that harm consisted in fundamentally opposing this interest. Harm to others shares the same basic framework, and similarly is a threat to or undermines such major interest. What constitutes such harm will to an extent depend on the relevant culture and on people's expectations of life's offerings. Technological and medical advances, for example, change people's expectations and thereby influence what they count as harm. But since 'harm to others' is here taken to be parallel to 'harm to oneself', it should be of so fundamental a nature that an examination of such contingencies would be irrelevant in the present context.

Some distinctions will, however, be useful for the discussion to follow. First, there are different kinds of harm. Most obviously, physical injury and the infliction of physical pain are likely to interfere, at least temporarily, with the person's ability to lead the sort of life she had planned for herself. Clearly, the range and degree of harm will extend over central as well as over marginal cases and will be more or less debatable. Psychological harm is similarly, though perhaps less obviously, a deprivation and interference with the person's normal functioning. Here the grey areas will be extensive, and decisions as to the nature and degree of harm caused more dependent on cultural and personal circumstances than in the case of physical harm. Considerations such as these apply also to what might be called 'moral harm', instances of which may be a person's deprivation of a clearly defined right, or, somewhat more nebulously, a failure in some respect to treat her as an 'end in herself'.

---

[1] David Wiggins discusses the relativity of harm in connection with need in 'Claims of Need', *Needs, Values, Truth* (Oxford: Basil Blackwell, 1987).

Cutting across these types of harm seen from the victim's point of view are further distinctions which introduce the agent into the picture. Harm may be inflicted on another deliberately or casually, negligently, with or without the agent being aware of causing harm. Sometimes the harm is only in intention and fails to be effective because the victim is too thick-skinned or too indifferent to experience it as harm, or may not share the agent's conception as to what constitutes an injury. But this is again a contingency which does not affect the vicious' potential impact on others. Certain types of harm to others can indeed be read off the characterization of all the vicious. Since their self-consciousness is always explicit, so that their experiences of the world are always experiences of themselves in the world, they are wholly self-centred. This must have its effect on the nature and degree of their awareness of the existence and consciousness of others, and so shape their attitude and behaviour towards them. Their personal relationships cannot be at all satisfactory, and at the very least they will tend to harm others through indifference, casually and without thought, an attitude likely, at least in certain circumstances, to be undermining of the other's self-esteem. Focusing their view on themselves in the world they will tend not to see the needs and sufferings of others even on those occasions when they could reasonably be expected to make them their concern. They are predisposed towards thoughtless cruelty and brutality.

It is of course not surprising that those who are preoccupied with themselves will fall short in their interest and care for others. A more challenging question is whether this or that vicious consciousness may also be disposed more positively towards harming others. If so, then this would go beyond merely shifting one's point of view from considering self-harm to thinking of them as potentially harming others. The predisposition towards cruelty and callousness through indifference is perhaps, at least in this or that individual vicious consciousness, a first step towards a more deliberate cruelty and callousness.

Cruelty is usually thought to be among if not the worst of all vices. Shklar, in her book *Ordinary Vices*, puts cruelty first. Montaigne confesses to a cruel hatred of cruelty, as the ultimate vice. The worst form, he thinks, is cruelty for the fun of it, when (as in hunting) ecstasy and rapture carry us away and reason is stunned (Essay, 'On

Cruelty'). In another Essay ('On Cowardice, the Mother of Cruelty') he speaks of a different type of cruelty, that of a tyrant which, he says, is based on fear. Hume comments that while the angry passions (anger and hatred) are always disagreeable, they are not necessarily vicious, but they are so 'when they rise up to cruelty; then they form the most detested of all vices' (*Treatise of Human Nature* 3. 3. 3). Aquinas discusses cruelty in connection with punishment: cruelty is nothing but hardness of heart in exacting punishment (*ST* 2a2ae q. 159 art. 1). He also thinks that it should be distinguished from brutality: 'a man who is angry without being hurt, or with one who has not offended him, is not said to be cruel, but to be brutal or savage' (ibid. q. 159 art. 2). In his view a man is cruel to another if, first, he perceives the other to have damaged him and wishes to retaliate, and secondly, he does so by damaging, or meaning to damage, the other more than the original offence merited. To retaliate cruelly is to punish unjustly. Aquinas thus gives cruelty a moral framework, thereby distinguishing it from brutality. This, he thinks is the behaviour of brutes, and a man who behaves brutally behaves in a manner which is sub-human.

It is Aquinas's distinction between cruelty and brutality rather than his setting within the area of punishment that points the way towards a more detailed characterization of the cruel. Retaliation does not seem decisive as a distinguishing mark, for not all cases of cruelty need be retaliatory, nor do all cases of brutality lack this desire. On the contrary, retaliation seems to feature more prominently in brutality than in cruelty, for at times at least the brutal appear to react precisely to some crippling damage they perceive as having been done to them, though neither the kind of damage itself nor its source may be clearly identifiable. It may be thought to be physical or psychological, the result of treatment by family, society, or state. Retaliation arising from perceptions of this sort is likely to be indiscriminate in the selection of its object. It may be quite accidental that some particular person (or thing) is the recipient of the aggression, an innocent victim of, perhaps, an excess of 'angry passions'. Alternatively the brutal may see their victim, if not personally responsible for the damage done to them, then as representative of those who are, and as such a proper object for revenge. So they may retaliate not for a specifiable harm done to them at some particular time by this or that particular person, but for some ongoing damage inflicted on them by some possibly not very clearly defined group which has prevented them from flourishing as they should.

The motivation for brutality is unlikely to be uniform and unmixed; the brutal may act in self-defence as well as in retaliation, perhaps to assert themselves in response to what they perceive as an insult. Similarly, cruelty may or may not be retaliatory. It may be precautionary, a move prompted by fear of possible harm in the future. This presumably was what Montaigne had in mind when citing the cruelty to his subjects of the tyrant afraid of possible rebellion. The cruel may act from fear but will also wish to impress on their victims their own superior position. They want to make their power felt, and inflicting suffering, or the fear of suffering, appears to them a promising means towards this end. So Machiavelli advises the Prince that cruelty is better than compassion, that, if one wants to maintain one's position of power, it is better to be feared than loved. Repeated acts of cruelty, or continuous expectation of being treated cruelly, will have a paralysing effect, and will reduce the person concerned to the status of a victim undermined in her capacity as an agent. The control over her actions is now in the hands of her tormentor, and this will enable him to regard her as dependent, powerless, and so altogether inferior.

Aquinas thinks of brutality as the savage treatment of some victim, apparently without cause, a type of behaviour which characterizes brutes rather than humans, so that when humans act brutally they act like animals. In this brutality differs from cruelty. This account points to an important distinction between the two, but before examining it two aspects of brutality have to be distinguished, namely, the brutal's state of mind or attitude towards his victim, and the manner in which his actions are carried out. The manner of acting is aggressively and conspicuously violent, and since so conspicuous and physical it tends to be the manner in which the harm is inflicted which we primarily think of in connection with brutality. The attitude is crude. Brutality is blinder, more unthinking than cruelty, and consequently more chancy and arbitrary. Its victims may be inanimate or sentient, and may be victims only accidentally, for the brutal have no interest in the individual person beyond perceiving in the potential victim those qualities or circumstances which make them obstacles, in one way or another, to their own well-being. A paradigm instance of both dimensions of brutality can be found in Dostoevsky's *Crime and Punishment*: Raskolnikov's murder of the rich old woman Alena Ivanova is brutal in its form of execution. He kills her by repeatedly hitting her over the head with a hatchet. His attitude towards her is that of the brutal, too, not only in its indifference towards her state and fate but also in its view of her: she, the worthless, wicked old woman, quite undeservedly and unfairly has the sort of wealth which he, the deserving and brilliant young student, needs and ought to have. She, and others like her in relevant respects, are in his way, are obstacles to his success. That is all he needs to know about her; she need not be further particularized or her fate be seen as a matter of concern; she is available for destruction, and this is enough to fasten on her as the victim (chs. 6 and 7).

The state of mind of the cruel is much more focused. They are concerned with their victim's feelings and responses as the brutal are not, and whose mark is rather uncaringness and total indifference towards the other's fate. The cruel, on the other hand, intend to harm the other for purposes of their own by producing certain negative reactions in him in ways which seem to them suitable in the circumstances. So, for instance, the means adopted may be brutal aggression, if this seems to them appropriate. But whatever the means adopted in pursuit of their aim, to achieve it they have to have, or have to think they have, some perception of the other's consciousness, or they would not be able to assess his reactions. Even if they, like the brutal, intend to cause physical damage, even if they behave in a brutal manner, the cruel person's interest is in the other's reaction to that damage. Cruelty may be more or less subtle, sophisticated, and discriminating, as brutality may not. Unlike brutality, cruelty always involves mental activity, in that the cruel but not the brutal need to ascribe a mental life to the potential victim and assess it from their particular point of view, which, in turn, requires thought on their own part. It is therefore quite plausible to suggest, as Aquinas does, that only one of the two vices may be regarded as based on attributes characteristic of persons.

The difference in the attitudes of the brutal and the cruel is reflected in the properties required to become a victim. The victim of brutality need only be available and destroyable. More is necessary for the victim of cruelty: not only has she to be capable of suffering, she should, for best effect, also be capable of remembering such suffering, and of formulating fearful expectations. Particular attempts at cruelty may therefore be more or less effective, depending on the potential victim's reaction to the particular treatment chosen. Mr Grandcourt, in George Eliot's *Daniel Deronda*, for instance, is a man given to cruelty but occasionally unlucky in the choice of his victims: he does not succeed in being cruel to his travel-companion and man of business, Mr Lush. He treats him like dirt, but Lush is thick-skinned, he knows where his bread is buttered and means to keep his position come what may. His love of ease is satisfied in his present position, 'and if his puddings were rolled towards him in the dust, he took the inside bits and found them relishing' (ch. 7). So he decides to regard his employer's attitude towards and treatment of him as a piece of eccentricity on that man's part, and as such not to be taken seriously. Luckily for Grandcourt, other victims are at hand. He fondles one of his dogs, Fluff, for the sole purpose, it seems, of causing his other dog, Fetch, to suffer: 'Grandcourt looked at her (Fetch) with unchanged face for half a minute, and then took the trouble to lay down his cigar while he lifted the unimpassioned Fluff close to his chin and gave it caressing pats, all the time gravely watching Fetch, who, poor thing, whimpered interruptedly' (ch. 12). Most importantly, his wife Gwendolen is the ideal victim, partly because she is the person she is, and partly because of the situation in which she finds herself. She is sensitive and imaginative; she has a strong desire for independence and a great deal of pride and some arrogance. She also knows that Grandcourt already has an illegitimate family, that consequently she ought not to have married him, that indeed in doing so she has broken a promise. Consequently she is guilt-ridden. Grandcourt knows her well enough to be aware of what for her would constitute almost unbearable humiliation, and he acts accordingly.

The cruel regard the other as something to be manipulated into a position of dependence through suffering and fear, thus destroying the victim's reasonable expectation of exercising a degree of control over her actions. Playing around with expectations is indeed among the tactics the cruel may employ. It adds spice to the other's suffering. Grandcourt, for instance, appears to encourage Gwendolen to hope that she might be allowed to visit her mother, only to dash this hope at a suitable moment. The view of the cruel as interfering with reasonable expectations is carried over to contexts where there is no human agency: a cruel fate is one that interferes with normal human expectations, or with well-founded hopes of the individual. A death, for instance, is thought particularly cruel if the age or apparent state of health of the person makes it a totally unexpected one. Again, as Aquinas pointed out, a punishment is cruel if the suffering inflicted is quite out of proportion with the crime committed, and so undeserved and not to be expected. Even assuming Gloucester to have been a traitor and as therefore deserving of punishment, the plucking out of his eyes cannot be seen as anything other than a piece of enormous cruelty. The very wording 'plucke out his eyes' implies Goneril's satisfaction as she envisages these means of causing extra suffering (William Shakespeare, *King Lear* III. vii. 6).

Deriving sadistic pleasure may play a part in the intention of the cruel, but it is unlikely to be the sole motivating force. Nor need there be any of the passions Hume refers to, or any occurrent emotion at all. Grandcourt for one remains totally cool and detached when engaged in his displays of cruelty. The underlying reasons for cruelty may, very roughly, be divided into reactive reasons and aggressive reasons. Reactive reasons are a response to some perceived suffering or humiliation on the agent's part, who sees his cruelty as a means towards getting his own back and re-establishing himself by reducing the status of the other. Aggressive reasons are precautionary in that the agent makes the first move in order to prevent a situation where she might find herself at the mercy of others. Central in either case is the agent's attempt to show the other his power to control, and this may or may not be accompanied by either pleasure, or by one or the other of the destructive emotions, or a mixture of them all.

Separating the agent's attitude towards the other from his manner of acting may make it hard or impossible to decide whether we have a case of cruelty or of brutality. The cruel may behave brutally and a brutal state of mind may not necessarily express itself in brutal physical aggression. Whether it is described as the one or the other will depend on how a particular case is understood. So, for instance, are the priest and the Levite brutal or cruel, or neither, when they pass by the man left half-dead by the roadside (Luke 10: 21)? They are certainly negligent and rather callous. Whether they are also either cruel or brutal depends on what one takes their attitude to be. They may be thought cruel if, being aware of the man's suffering, they deliberately ignore it and consequently interfere with the reasonable expectation he may have had that help was on the way. They may even positively approve of his helplessness as a mark of his inferiority to them. This would link their attitude to standard cases of cruelty. But their attitude may also be thought brutal in its callous indifference towards the man's state; he is merely an obstacle in their way which can be removed without physical violence by simply ignoring it. They see no reason why their plans should in any way be altered by the needs of another. This type of negative aggression is evident also in cases that may be regarded as mental brutality, where, without using physical violence, what is callously and indifferently destroyed are the other's wants and feelings.

Cruelty and brutality were introduced as prominent cases of harmful attitudes towards others in order to see whether individual vices are 'capital' with regard to either or both of these. The question now is whether this or that vice has characteristics which will predispose its possessor to cruel or brutal treatment of others, whether a tendency towards brutality or cruelty is consequent upon the possession of this or that deadly vice, and is one that goes beyond the indifference towards others which, since they are wholly self-centred, is built into the vicious' disposition. Their constant pursuance of unfulfillable and inward-directed desires alienates them from their surroundings and, depending on the specific nature of their perspective on the world, distances them from others.

It was particularly the arrogantly proud who assumed and desired such a distance. Nothing, in their view, could be more presumptuous than the attempt by others to narrow it and thereby to threaten their uniquely superior position. Any potential usurper must be repressed and possibly punished. While it does not follow necessarily that they will react either cruelly or brutally, their perception of the other's impertinence and their need to reimpress their superiority are promising foundations for either, and make the corresponding reaction a natural one. Treatment of the other in such circumstances may be brutal, if he is seen as merely a tiresome and offensive obstacle to be got rid of. Or it may be cruel, if the proud see themselves as inflicting well-deserved punishment by means of which they wish the victim to have to acknowledge their superiority and control.

The assumption of distance between himself and others enables
the proud to trivialize their needs, wants, and feelings, so that it is an
easy step for him either to totally ignore or else to manipulate the
others' interests for purposes of his own. It is this assumption which
predisposes the proud towards a callousness which may amount to
brutality or cruelty in certain circumstances. In the perception of the
envious there, too, is such a distance between himself and others, but
conversely, here it is the envious who see themselves as in some way
inferior. It is this perception which makes them the most obvious
candidates predisposed towards causing positive harm, for aggression
is built into the structure of the vice in the form of the desire to
destroy the other's occupation of the supposedly superior position.
In circumstances where they are able to act on such desires they, too,
may do so either brutally or cruelly, depending on how interested
they are in the reaction of the envied person herself. They may
conceivably not care about that at all, being concerned only with
their relative standing in their own eyes and in that of the world. On
the other hand, it may be that the other's suffering itself constitutes
or is part of the desired reversal of their respective positions. Her
satisfaction with her status may have been at least a contributary
source of their envy, and so is something to be undermined. More
straightforwardly, wishing to see the other suffer may also be a desire
for revenge, for the pleasure of paying back those seen as in some
way responsible for one's own misery. That would be an expression
of resentment, an emotion naturally felt by the envious. Cruelty
seems a particularly suitable weapon for those whose self-image is
damaged, for thinking of oneself as being able to exercise power
over another may well appear a most effective way of establishing or
re-establishing a more positive view of oneself. Both the envious and
the resentful need their self-image to be enhanced, and consequently
both are predisposed towards reactive cruelty.

Aggression, though not of an openly hostile kind, is characteristic
also of the lustful. Typically at least these are not out to cause
suffering and so they are not typically cruel. It is true that they wish
for power, but seeing this in sexual success they need not induce
the fear of suffering for their desire to be satisfied, or at any rate
need not do so if they are reasonably accomplished seducers. It is
true also that to achieve their aim some manipulation of the other

may be required, but this again would be incidental to rather than part of the plan. But while neither cruel nor necessarily predisposed towards cruelty, the lustful are plainly brutal in their attitude and treatment of others, for like the brutal they do not see them as individuals at all, and are indifferent to any emotions and hopes they may arouse. They are brutal also in their behaviour towards those who, their hopes and emotions aroused, imagine themselves involved in a proper relationship. The classic example here is Don Giovanni's treatment of Donna Elvira, whose real feelings and fidelity are a threat to his fantasy life.

It can be said, then, of the proud, the envious, resentful, and lustful that the desire-structure of their relevant vice is such that, in various ways, they are predisposed towards agressive behaviour which is harmful to others. This is true also of the miserly avaricious. The reason is that the miser views the world with suspicion and sees others as hostile, a threat to what she treasures. Such a perception of the world may well provoke violent aggression at times, either deliberately because seen as a piece of necessary self-defence, or as a reaction simply to feelings of fear. On such occasions their perspective is that of the brutal rather than the cruel. They do not primarily wish to assert themselves by means of manipulating others; rather, they wish to remove what interferes with their dedication to their lifestyle.

The misers' feeling of insecurity may also in other ways prompt such aggression: since they are likely to feel that the larger their store the better rooted their security, their miserliness may be accompanied by greed, and they may be constantly on the lookout for means of increasing their hoard. The greedier they become the more ruthless they will tend to be in the pursuance of their goal. But greed is not restricted to their case: other vices, too, are characterized by greed, not merely for money, food and drink, or sex, but also for admiration and recognition. It may have been the thought that the vicious are all ruthless in their greed which was in Aquinas's mind when he offered his definition of a capital sin in terms of adopting immoral means in order to achieve a passionately desired end. It is from this point of view, but only from this point of view, that the glutton may be said to be predisposed towards harmful treatment of others; his specific view of the world and consequent desires offer no other pointer, except of course that he, like the others, will tend to react violently against anyone who may attempt to interfere with his chosen course.

The slothful alone appear to be free from greed. Their disengagement from the world prevents them from pursuing any aim with any degree of determination, and usually prevents them also from having any particular interest in harming another. The very nature of its deadliness seems to prevent sloth from being a capital vice, except that the slothful, like all the vicious, are negligent in their attitude towards others, and so may well strike the other as being cruel or brutal. Under certain conditions they may also be said to be predisposed towards the cruelty (or brutality) of indifference, this being consequent upon precisely their inability to commit themselves: the circumstances of ordinary life being what they are, they are almost bound to find themselves in situations where commitment on their part is to be expected, but such expectations will remain unfulfilled. Oblomov's behaviour towards Olga displays such cruelty: he has given her grounds for expecting a lasting relationship, but being unable to face this prospect he withdraws. Yet he cannot even commit himself to the sentiments expressed in his letter of farewell, and so he meets her again only, she has reason to believe, in order to see her weep (Ivan Goncharov, *Oblomov*, ch. 10). For even a kindly man such as Oblomov, cruelty of this type is inevitable when the slothful enter some sort of personal relationship, for fulfilling the requirements of such a relationship demands qualities of a kind they do not possess. There is further the possibility that, in certain circumstances, they use cruel treatment of another as a means towards an end: the bored have to find some way of filling the time that is on their hands, and exercising power over others may be a relatively amusing way of doing so. Mr Grandcourt in his treatment of Fetch and of his wife seems to be partially motivated by a search for amusement of precisely this kind.

All the vicious, including the slothful, are vulnerable to attack, and self-defence and self-protection afford strong motivation for violence against others. The slothful may so react if shown that there is perhaps something worth engaging with, the envious when they meet reminders that their self-image needs enhancing, the proud when it seems necessary to impress the validity of theirs on others. Violent reaction to an attack on one's status and way of life is no doubt a common occurrence and not confined to the vicious, but their basic anxieties and insecurities which have to be hidden from themselves make their position a particularly vulnerable one. Their self-deceptive self-protection will tend to make them be on the lookout for anything that might pierce their armour, and tend to make them perceive attacks where none were intended. This in turn will incline them to ascribe hostility-provoking properties to others which may be wholly fantasy-based or be at any rate exaggerated, and thereby confirm and widen the distance between them. The self-defeating and constantly frustrating nature of their self-directed desires is reflected in this ever-widening distance from others, perpetually renewing and encouraging their anxieties, and so preparing the ground for violent reaction.

The self-deception of the vicious, needed to protect themselves from disturbing realizations about themselves, has itself to be protected from discovery by others, and so plays a part in predisposing them towards aggression. It does so also in another way. The vicious' self-deception means that they present a false self to the world. In that sense they are hypocrites. They are not, or need not be, hypocritical in its most obvious way; they do not, Tartuffe-like, knowingly and cynically set out to deceive others about their aims and convictions. Since it reflects the nature and degree of their self-deception it is a more deeply rooted hypocrisy, which in itself is an obstacle to any genuine personal relationship and thus contributes to the distance between themselves and others. But further, what they do to themselves is reflected in what they do to others. Their layer of self-deception is corruptive of the self. The layer of protection against others is similarly corruptive of their relationship with others. This may mean merely that they withdraw and isolate themselves. But there will also be the tendency to see their (self-imposed) frustrations as the result of destructive attitudes and behaviour on the part of others. In that case concealed self-destruction is projected unto others and seen as a hostility which needs to be warded off by retaliatory destruction. While from their point of view this is an attractive move since it absolves the vicious themselves from responsibility for their condition, it also deepens the sense of anxiety which stems from the suspected insecurity of their position.

Sartre's play *Huis Clos* encapsulates some of the connections between anxiety about maintaining one's ill-founded but cherished self-image and the consequent impossibility of entering into some form of personal relationship. Three characters, recently dead, experience hell through unavoidable torturing of each other. They cannot avoid doing so since they are unable to present themselves to others as they wish to be seen, and as they wish to see themselves. Estelle, vain and used to admiration, is lost when she discovers that there are no mirrors available. She depends on them: 'When I talked to people I always made sure there was one near by in which I could see myself. I watched myself talking. And somehow it kept me alert, seeing myself as the others saw me . . .'[2] But what she sees is her own image as she perceives it to be seen by an admiring world. She is deceiving herself. The mirror is needed not to show her how others see her, but to provide her with a flattering self-image, and it is this which keeps her alert and which is needed for her to live with herself. Her reflection in the glass, as she herself puts it, is a 'tamed' one. When Inez, a former post-office clerk with no experience of Estelle's social world and its customs, offers to be her mirror, it will not do at all. Far from seeing Estelle as a 'glancing stream' or 'crystal girl' she alleges that her mouth looks cruel and that she has a nasty red spot. Even when Inez attempts to play the game her role is not accepted by Estelle, for Inez's inferior position does not qualify her for it. She does not belong to the world that matters, and is in any case not a man but a lesbian whose advances are distasteful to her. Any attempt to extract the desired response from Garcin, the only available man, also ends in failure, for Estelle, looking for nothing but flattery, has herself nothing but flattery to give, and her version of it is of no use to the intellectual Garcin. With no response from him, an inadequate one from Inez, and her former admirers on earth beginning to forget her, her favourable self-image cannot be kept alive and 'the crystal's shattered into bits' (p. 210).

Inez on her part is aware of herself as an outsider, both in the world she came from where she felt ignored or despised by those who, like Estelle and Garcin, were her social superiors; and again here, where it seems that a liaison between Estelle and Garcin will

---

[2] Jean-Paul Sartre, *In Camera*, tr. Stuart Gilbert (London: Penguin, 1988), 197.

shut her out. She is full of resentment and envy, is indeed in the grip of what Scheler called 'existential envy', which cannot forgive others that they are what they are.[3] She ruthlessly uses her weapon of disparaging the self-image the other two wish to project, refusing not only to give Estelle the reassurance of her identity she longs for, but also to take seriously Garcin's attempt to present himself as something of a hero who was executed because he courageously lived up to his noble principles. Both he and Estelle are preoccupied with their self-image, both want to shine in ways which are relevant to their respective positions in life. Both are vain and arrogant, and for them hell consists in the destruction of admirable Estelle and courageous Garcin through lack of the 'right' response from the others. Inez, by contrast, is aware that she is far from admirable. As she remarks, she cannot get on without making people suffer, when she is alone she flickers out. Although she speaks disparagingly of herself ('I'm rotten to the core') she has taken pride in her very destructiveness. Her torture is the realization that her pride in herself is a hollow one, and that she will have to live forever and ever with that envy-embedded self. 'Hell is other people' says Garcin at the end of the play. It is hell for those who, like the characters in the play, have nourished themselves on a deceptive self-image and are now forced to see it disappear.

[3] For a discussion of the play, and in particular of Inez as an embodiment of *ressentiment*, see Rhiannon Goldthorpe, *Sartre: Literature and Theory* (Cambridge: Cambridge University Press, 1984), ch. 3, '*Huis Clos*: Distance and Ambiguity'.

8 COUNTERVAILING VIRTUES

I

IN their attitude towards themselves the vicious are self-destructive. A countervailing virtue should then be in some way a good to that self; where the vices destroy and corrupt, a countervailing virtue should heal and hold the self together. Such 'self-healing' virtues are not necessarily what might be regarded as strictly 'moral' virtues, which require some form of altruistic motivation. The possessor of a countervailing virtue need not be a generous, charitable, or just person. But nor do they necessarily belong to that class sometimes labelled 'self-regarding' and sometimes 'executive' virtues, which an agent may exercise for either her own or someone else's benefit, so that a person may possess all these virtues and yet be wholly self-interested and even wicked.[1] Courage, prudence, patience, and self-control belong to this class. While a self-healing virtue will be seen to connect with both these other types, its main point is that it offers the agent a manner of escape from the burden of his or her self which provides him or her with the opportunity of leading a happier life. The emphasis here is on the *manner* of escape, for escape from the burden of oneself can perhaps be seen as the driving force behind the attitudes and actions of the vicious. But there the attempted escape was in the wrong direction.

---

[1] E.g. G. H. von Wright, *The Varieties of Goodness* (London: Routledge and Kegan Paul, 1953), divides virtues into self- and other-regarding. Bernard Williams, in *Ethics and the Limits of Philosophy* (London: Fontana, 1985), speaks of 'executive' virtues. If, as on the Aristotelian view, all virtues require practical wisdom, then the 'courage' or 'prudence' exercised for unworthy ends would not be proper courage etc. at all; *Nicomachean Ethics*, bk. 3.

The starting-point for the consideration of countervailing virtues is yet again the nature of the vicious' self-consciousness. Their self-centredness was seen to be naturally reflected in their attitude towards others. In different ways and to different degrees they can all be described as moral solipsists: their self-preoccupation is complemented by other-indifference. As the discussion of individual vices has shown, the vicious, while of course aware that there are other agents in their universe with, apparently, aims of their own, fail to acknowledge these as agents in their own right. For them they exist only in so far as they affect their own lives. The slothful find them no more interest-engaging than they find themselves; for the glutton they need be nothing but providers of the food he enjoys or the nourishment he needs. Similarly, the vain and conceited see them merely as necessary for the fulfilment of their specific desires. The arrogant are altogether indifferent, and concerned only when they perceive offensive lack of recognition of their superiority, while the lustful's interest in others is restricted to a narrow range of reactions to himself. For the resentful, envious, and avaricious they are a source of harm to themselves. Since moral solipsism of this kind and self-corruption are two sides of the same coin, a countervailing virtue will prevent or modify the one as well as the other. Self-healing requires removal of the other-indifference inherent in the position of those in the grip of a vice.

The vicious do not value themselves. They lack self-esteem, self-respect, perhaps self-love. These will be healing virtues all of them require. But possessing these to even some degree entails abandoning their solipsistic position. I shall approach the examination of suitable virtues from this latter angle.

The moral solipsist fails to acknowledge others as persons in their own right. His awareness of their states of consciousness is severely biased and restricted, and any feelings he may have which both influence and respond to this awareness are wholly self-referential feelings. Since he feels only for himself, any personal relationship with another is doomed from the start. To acknowledge others, therefore, both awareness of their consciousness and any feeling involved should at least occasionally be self-transcendent.

Awareness and feeling may be said to be 'self-transcendent' if their focus is some object other than the self. This characterization allows self-transcendent perception and feeling to have a range of 'objects', including but not restricted to other human beings. The agent may concentrate such feelings on friends and family, or alternatively on some cause or enterprise which engages his interests and talents. At present the focus is taken to be another person. There are degrees of self-transcendence. Minimally it requires a shift in a person's point of view away from the entirely self-referential one. For this to be possible at all the agent in question must be capable of being aware that another has views and attachments because of which certain events or actions will affect her (the other) in certain ways. The possibility of such a minimal imaginative leap is a precondition for self-transcendence; it may or may not be the first step to self-transcendence itself. There is no reason to deny the moral solipsist such minimal capacity. The vicious, if intent on certain types of self-defence or revenge, will indeed make use of this ability. But this does not amount to self-transcendence. The reason is that the shift of view and its nature are themselves dictated wholly by the self-referential desires and interests of the person concerned. The other is still seen as being of importance merely because of the relation she has to the agent himself, so that the perspective within which the shift takes place remains the original self-centred one. The agent's attention may be on the other, but his interest is for himself alone and determines the precise location of the attention. Any desires he has are basically I-desires, although these may be overlaid by sets of non-I-desires.

A condition for self-transcendence must therefore be that the other's envisaged response to the world is not to be seen from a perspective which regards her as existing merely in relation to the agent himself. Such a perspective, being impregnated with self-referential feelings, cannot be one that he can share with the other, who naturally will not see the situation in this light. He must therefore, to whatever degree that may be possible, dissociate himself from feelings of that kind if he is to understand at all her views and her response. He needs at least some basic kind of sympathy.

Hume thought of sympathy as that feeling without which we could have no morality at all, and he is right if taken to mean that without some form of it there could be no moral agents capable of grasping the nature of values. The basic form of sympathy which I think he has in mind is the ability to represent to oneself the mental state of others irrespective of one's own interests, a feat which evidently is not possible if one is chained to one's self-referential perspective. It is the kind of imagination here needed which is lacking in the vicious, and this lack is reflected in their view of themselves as well as in their view of others. For, not acknowledging others as being persons in their own right, they cannot imaginatively grasp possible alternative perceptions of or feeling-responses to a given state of affairs; in their self-absorption they cannot see the situation in any way other than they actually do. This is one reason why there cannot in them be a shift towards a relatively detached view of the self—which accounts for the stubbornness with which the vicious persist in their ways.

Representing another's state of mind to oneself does not by itself ensure the experience of positive feelings towards that other: one may remain detached, indifferent, or even hostile. While no longer a moral solipsist, the agent concerned may still be a misanthrope, and so hardly to be described as a sympathetic person. Sympathy as it is usually understood requires more. There should be some feeling-reaction, some form of feeling with the other.

The phenomenon of 'feeling with . . .' covers a wide range of different cases. At one end of the scale 'feeling with' carries little emotional content but is expressed primarily in action. This is probably the type of sympathy we tend to expect of members of the caring professions: the nurse feels with her patient in that representing to herself the other's state of mind she sees that something should be done about it. She does not (and probably should not) feel what her patient feels; she is not infected by the feeling. Being infected, i.e. feeling pain because the other does, or joy because the other does, is a case of 'feeling with' at the other end of the scale. This type of feeling may be appropriate on certain sorts of occasions, but it is also associated with a variety of dangers. Scheler (*Ressentiment*, p.12) gives as an example of the crudest form of such undesirable infection the behaviour of people in a crowd, where, seeing some angry, alarmed, or frightened, others also experience these emotions. His point here is that being infected by the emotions of others need not mean that the others' state of mind is understood at all. The representation of the other's state of mind becomes irrelevant, each member of the crowd being concerned with their own feelings only, so that this type of infection is a 'feeling with' which cannot be regarded as being proper sympathy at all.

In friendship, and generally in personal relationships, we tend to expect a type of sympathy which includes but goes beyond that which is appropriate to members of the caring professions. We expect a more emotional reaction, but hope for better understanding of our states of mind than would be needed if our emotions were merely to infect the other. Sympathy here means that the representation of the other's state of mind is crucial in affecting the person's emotional reaction, so that she vicariously feels the same. The feeling is 'the same' only in the sense that it is the same sort of feeling: joy if the other's state of mind is a joyful one, some form of pain if it is painful. But in other ways it is of course different, not only in that it is felt by another person, but less obviously so because its 'object' is different. The initial joy was felt in direct response to some happening or situation; sympathetic joy is only obliquely so connected, but is more directly a response to the first state of joy. It is the other's state of mind which this joy is primarily about. Similar considerations apply to sympathy with painful states of mind, but there is here also a difference which makes feeling joy and feeling pain with the other different sorts of sympathy: the latter requires a concern to at least try and alleviate the pain in some way which is not in place in the other case. If that is lacking, sympathy with pain will tend to lapse into that kind of 'feeling with' which was an infection of feeling and not proper sympathy at all. It is this danger which led some philosophers to think feeling pain with others a wholly bad thing, being no more than a rather morbid kind of suffering or fear for oneself.[2] Feeling sympathetic joy, on the other hand, can hardly be anything other than a wholly generous feeling. Both types of (proper) sympathy are components of personal love.

Basic sympathy, the ability to represent to oneself another's state of consciousness beyond the merely self-referential context, is necessary for the avoidance of moral solipsism. It opens the possibility not only of other-regarding concern, but also of proper engagement in practical reasoning. It enables the agent to grasp the distinction between relatively subjective and objective viewpoints, and thereby also provides him with the means of distinguishing between values and mere preferences. Basic sympathy is thus necessary for the possession

---

[2] Max Scheler, *Ressentiment* (New York: Schocken, 1972), discusses various misunderstandings in detail.

of a self-healing virtue. More is required if it is to be regarded as a virtue, for basic sympathy is compatible with a range of negative reactions. To provide motivation for its positive use and guarantee its healing impact on the agent, basic sympathy must be complemented by self-transcendent feeling. Such feelings are involved in a fuller form of sympathy, but are particularly so in personal love, and it is love which is prominent among the candidates for the status of being a healing virtue. The role of love is further given particular relevance to the present context by the doctrine that vice is love perverted in various ways. Unlike sympathy, love is among those psychic feelings which may be self-directed as well as self-transcendent, and so the question arises whether vice may be thought to exhibit a perversion of it precisely because love is here self-directed, or whether it is the specific form of self-love which constitutes the perversion, while in another form it may itself be a self-healing virtue. The brief examination of love which follows is, of course, by no means to be regarded as an exhaustive one, but is intended merely to highlight its remedial properties.

Love, whether or not it includes sexual desire, is at any rate not just sexual desire. Hume occasionally seems to take it in just this sense. In his Essay 'on Love and Marriage' he links love with pleasure only and suggests that it never looks beyond present momentary gratification, or the satisfying of a prevailing inclination. This is clearly a wholly inadequate account. Kant offers a more acceptable proposal. It is of course often pointed out—and frequently held against him—that Kant dismisses what he calls 'pathological love' altogether and recommends merely 'practical love', which, he says, is a duty. If by 'practical love' he means 'assisting others on the basis of sympathy in the sense of being able to represent to oneself another's state of mind without thereby being infected by the other's feelings' then this view on its own has much to recommend it. But Kant has more to say on this topic, in contexts where he is concerned with the substance rather than the foundations of morality. In his lecture on self-love he speaks of love of another as the delight we take in his perfection. He also discusses the love in friendship.[3] While he here emphasizes that

---

[3] *Metaphysics of Morals*, pt. II; *Metaphysical Principles of Virtue*, pt. I; *Elements of Ethics*, para. 46.

love in friendship cannot be entirely left to feelings since these alone cannot guard against breaches of friendship, feelings themselves are given an important role: in love there is a 'sweetness of sensation which approximates a fusion into one person'.

Kant points in the right direction, I think, in the features of personal love he mentions. Delight in the other's existence is a positive feeling-state in the complex of relevant feelings. It is a feeling which both expresses a valuing of the other and is of value in itself, not just, or not primarily, because it is a pleasant feeling, but because it is an enriching one. One's life is the richer because there is the other and because one is able to appreciate fully this existence. Delight in the other's existence is a feeling on its own, to be distinguished from both feelings for and feelings with the other. The lover feels for the other by being interested in, being concerned about, and caring for her. He also, at least to a degree, feels with the other, in the sense of sharing her feelings as described earlier. This makes love not merely a self-transcendent but also a participatory feeling (or cluster of feelings), which may account for the sense of identification and union referred to by Kant. Love therefore breaks down the isolation consequent on wholly self-directed feelings.

Kant speaks of delight as being in the other's perfection. Maybe he is thinking of the rational or good man's love, which is not superficial but will include character and value. If the suggestion is that in general we love another because we see certain (moral?) perfections in him then it is a rather dubious point. Love is rarely so motivated. More plausibly it might be said that it is in the nature of love to ascribe to the other certain perfections. It is no doubt true that often, at least in personal love, the other's image is an idealized one and his or her value plain to the lover only. But whether or not the beloved is seen as having certain perfections, the presence of feelings of the kind enumerated clearly implies that the lover sets store by the object of her love, that she thinks it worth her while to engage in the efforts of attention directed towards it, that she will endeavour to get to know the other. The extension of feeling thereby involves a general expansion of consciousness. She will also be concerned about the other's attitude towards herself. If her love is returned she will feel herself valued, and in any case, she values being valued by the other. But while this is an important ingredient of loving another, the nature of the concern and expectation on the lover's part concerning the other's attitude towards herself covers a very wide range. In what Robert Solomon[4] calls 'romantic love' there is no doubt the desire for intimacy, for shared passion and tenderness, and the withdrawal of the other's love may well be the greatest threat. But this is only one type of case. Still, in all but the most self-sacrificing types of love, the lover wants at least to be acknowledged as having some importance in the other's life. Dependence, to a degree, on another's evaluation of oneself will affect one's self-evaluation. It forces the agent to shift her point of view and so at least makes possible a better knowledge of herself. Self-transcendence is the basic step necessary for gaining a self-knowledge that is substantial, possibly through the route suggested by Aristotle: since we are in a better position to discern and assess another's character rather than our own where partiality tends to make us blind, reflection on and comparison with that character should make us better acquainted with our own (*Nicomachean Ethics* 1169^{b}28–1170^{a}4).[5] Whether or not this is achieved will depend on the nature of the love looked for and received. Its self-transcendence does not of course imply that love may not be defective (e.g. in its demands on the other) or that it must bring more happiness than sorrow. It implies merely that love is positive and participatory, and so expands one's universe. In practice, whether some person loves another or merely makes her part of his self-centred universe may be hard or impossible to say. Defective love and solipsistic narcissism may appear indistinguishable.

There can be no simple symmetry between love of oneself and love of another: while it may make good sense to feel *for* oneself, it is hard to see what feeling *with* oneself might amount to. A participatory feeling cannot be wholly self-directed. Self-love, it would seem, cannot be an enriching emotion which expands one's consciousness. Again, it may be possible to take delight in one's own existence, but hardly in the same way as one takes delight in the existence of

---

[4] Robert C. Solomon, 'The Virtue of Love', *Midwest Studies in Philosophy* 13, *Ethical Theory: Character and Virtue* (1988), 12–31.

[5] For a discussion of Aristotle's claim see Martha Nussbaum, *The Fragility of Goodness* (Cambridge: Cambridge University Press, 1986), ch. 11; and Julia Annas, *The Morality of Happiness* (Oxford: Oxford University Press, 1993), ch. 12.

another. Kant, speaking in terms of perfection, proposes that the love which takes delight in others is the *judgement* of delight in their perfection, while the love which takes delight in ourselves, or self-love, is an *inclination* to be well-content with ourselves in judging our own perfection. Needless to say, Kant takes a poor view of this kind of self-love. In his account it is a partiality towards oneself for which there cannot be any reason. It is a form of arrogance. The partiality of this type of self-love (Kant calls it 'Eigenliebe') is to be contrasted with a partiality inherent in another kind ('Selbstliebe'), where it is unavoidable and not a vice. Self-love here is a form of that benevolence which we have a duty to practice towards everyone. But 'everyone' includes ourselves. As Kant says, extensively a general (practical) love of mankind is the greatest possible benevolence, but intensively it is the smallest possible. Benevolence towards people means taking an interest in them, but the 'interest' may range over being just not indifferent to being intensely involved. 'One person may be closer to me than another;' Kant says, 'and I am the one closest to myself as far as benevolence is concerned' (*Elements of Ethics*, para. 28). That I therefore should particularly look after myself and my nearest and dearest is only to be expected. Doing so, Kant claims, is consistent with fulfilling the duty of general benevolence.

Kant, then, allowed for a certain partiality in one's attitude towards oneself. Such self-love, while not a vice, is of course not a virtue either, it is just a fact about human nature which cannot be ignored. Kant does not discuss the ways in which this kind of self-love also may go wrong, or even consider that it may do so.[6] But clearly it may get out of hand in that one's self-concern may be totally out of proportion with one's concern for others. While the agent will not exhibit the total self-centredness which marks the moral solipsist, she may still tend to be selfish in that, though in her practical reasoning she does not ignore the claims of others altogether, she still may weight different claims heavily in her own favour. But here, as ever, borderlines are blurred. If she consistently thinks of self-regarding reasons as outweighing other-regarding ones then her reference to

---

[6] He does not do so, presumably, because this type of self-love is ascribed to a rational human being, and Kant may have thought that the rationality includes the weighting of reasons.

others may well be thought to be at best only superficially sincere. Kant's two kinds of self-love are therefore not as cleanly to be seperated as he apparently assumed.

Nevertheless, his basic thought seems clear enough, and his distinction between the judgement of delight and the inclination to be well-contented can be taken to indicate a way in which true and false self-love may, at least theoretically, be distinguished from one another. For Kant, a judgement of delight is not merely about the subject's own state; it demands a degree of disinterestness, and the emotional reaction of delight has some objective backing. It does not express a mere liking or preference but is based on a perception of something worth taking delight in. 'Inclination', on the other hand, is purely subjective, lacking all detachment and objectivity. Such an inclination to feel content with oneself cannot be based on any assessment of whether one may be right to feel that way. Self-love of this type is then indeed at best a smug self-satisfaction, and at worst a form of vicious pride.

Uncritical self-satisfaction is one kind of false self-love. Another type is self-indulgence, the opting for easy pleasures and facile solutions. It, like self-satisfaction, is quite uncritical and does not involve proper evaluations. It, too, is 'inclination'- and not 'judgement'-based. On the other hand, self-indulgence need not be accompanied by self-satisfaction; it is on the contrary compatible with dislike of and even contempt for oneself. Slothful Oblomov and gluttonous Mrs Clenham were self-indulgent, but neither of them had a particular liking for him- or herself. This indeed was part of their trouble. But a self-love which is compatible with such hostile feelings towards oneself can hardly be thought of as a good to its possessor. In a sophisticated form it is the self-love predominantly exhibited by the vicious. Their chief indulgence, as we have seen, is to protect the self from painful discoveries.

A genuine self-love, one which is self-healing and self-enriching and is in this sense a virtue, would seem to have to parallel the love of another at any rate in this respect, that it has as one of its constituents a delight in one's own existence which is not uncritical but is the response to seeing it as being of value. This means that it is a self-love which depends on acknowledging the status of others. This is so because, first, valuing something requires more

than reliance on inclination and personal preference, but since the
solipsist cannot have proper values, this is all he is capable of. He
therefore cannot properly value himself (see Ch. 5). Secondly, it
seems psychologically hardly possible to value oneself without the
belief that one is valued by others. At least part of the worth seen in a
beloved is in perceiving him as a possible source for this belief. Since
the agent capable of love has some conception of value, and since she
is not out to protect and reassure herself come what may, she will not
be inclined to accept any piece of flattery as an expression of regard,
and this again means that she cannot think of the other as existing
only in so far as he can be of service to her. For both conceptual and
psychological reasons, then, genuine self-love cannot be had without
some acknowledgement of others as persons in their own right.
Self-transcendence is consequently a necessary condition for such
self-love. But self-love can also be said to be itself a self-transcendent
feeling. It is not of course a feeling directed towards others, but it is
still self-transcendent in the basic sense, in that it is not the self on
which it is primarily focused. The relevant agent's self-consciousness
cannot be a wholly explicit one, concentrating merely on her status in
the world, for that is precisely the position which can be accompanied
by only self-satisfaction or self-indulgence. Genuine self-love, since it
rests on positive self-evaluation, demands that the person concerned
should feel herself to be engaged with the world in ways which she
considers to be worthwhile. It is these engagements rather than she
herself which will absorb her attention.

The parallel between love of another and genuine self-love can,
then, be pushed a little further: in self-love the identification with
another is paralleled by identification with one's occupations; in both
cases it entails the (temporary) forgetting of one's own existence,
of *oneself* as doing this or that. A difference in focus is likely to
bring with it certain other consequent differences. Love of another,
I suggested, has among its elements feelings of delight in the other's
existence. But feeling delight at one's own existence seems, at least
at first sight, to be at variance with self-forgetfulness and to be
akin rather to self-satisfaction. But this is not so if it is taken to be
the feeling of being alive generated by the interest taken in one's
activities and the pleasure of a sense of achievement. Neither of these
are expressions of self-concern or necessarily of self-satisfaction.

Both love of another and genuine self-love are healing virtues, but it is self-love which is most relevant to the plight of the vicious. From this point of view its most important element is the sense of self-worth which it entails, a self-worth which has at least a degree of relative objectivity. It shares features with the type of pride often thought to be a virtue, of which Hume says that 'nothing is more useful to us in the conduct of life, than a due degree of pride, which makes us sensible of our own merit, and gives us a confidence and assurance in all our projects and enterprizes' (*Treatise of Human Nature*, bk. 3, pt. 3, sect. 2). Hume makes the here crucially relevant point that it is the agent himself to whom such virtuous pride is of benefit, but often it, like self-respect, is taken to have also more specifically moral implications. Pride taken as the self-regarding version of respect for others will prevent a person from doing what he regards as shameful or dishonourable; he will know what is due to himself as well as what is due to others.[7] Such implications go beyond what is required for the possession of a self-healing virtue. 'Self-esteem' is perhaps a more suitable label, in that it indicates more directly than does 'proper pride' or 'self-respect' a positive attitude towards ourselves, which, as Hume says, generates a degree of self-confidence, and this in turn will positively affect our attitudes towards the projects we are engaged with.[8] The possession of self-esteem would then make unnecessary the constant search for self-protection to which the vicious were condemned.

With diminishing need for self-protection there is a diminishing need also for that web of self-deception in which the vicious were entangled. Some degree of a certain type of honesty would then seem to be a healing virtue which is consequent upon the healing virtue of self-love or self-esteem. Honesty covers a wide range of types of case, not all of which are relevant here. A distinction may be drawn between 'inner' and 'outer' aspects of honesty. 'Outer' refers to those

---

[7] See e.g. Casey, *Pagan Virtue* (Oxford: Oxford University Press, 1990), ch. 1, sect. vi.

[8] In his Introduction to the collection of articles *Dignity, Character and Self-Respect*, (New York: Routledge, 1995), the editor, Robin S. Dillon, summarizes the different interpretations offered by both philosophers and psychologists of 'self-respect' and 'self-esteem'. As he points out, moral philosophers tend to speak of self-respect, psychologists of self-esteem.

characteristics in virtue of which a person is judged to be honest by others: an honest person behaves 'honourably', she will not deceive, she can be trusted. The 'inner' aspect is not parallel, for it does not refer to characteristics in virtue of which the agent herself sees herself as honest. Instead it refers to her 'inner' attitude and reasoning, to how she deals with her life irrespective of whether questions as to her trustworthiness arise. A degree of such honesty is needed for the assessment of the more or less worthwhile. It is countervailing to the tendency to attach more or less weight to reasons for action depending only on how conveniently they do or do not fit into a (self-protective) system of beliefs and desires. It requires a relative objectivity, a clear-sightedness on the part of the agent about what it is important for her to identify with. This clear-sightedness may have been in Aquinas's mind when he equated honesty with spiritual beauty, which 'consists in a man's conduct or actions being well proportioned in respect of the spiritual clarity of reason' (*Summa Theologiae* (*ST*) 2a2ae, q. 145 art. 2). As was pointed out earlier (Ch. 4), such clarity in assessment and reasoning is constituent of self-knowledge and hence opposed to self-deception. It results in the agent's conviction about the relative merits of the values perceived, and of the possibilities open to her, and not in only unstable feelings of conviction. This is implied by the perception being of a value, and not of merely a preference, a 'value' she has created through her own desires.

II

The 'healing virtues' discussed so far are evidently virtues corrective of all the vices. Nothing has as yet been said about individual virtues which may correspond to this or that specific vice. There seem to be at least some quite obvious couples: pride and humility or modesty; gluttony and temperance; lust and chastity; wrath and patience; sloth and industry. Temperance, chastity, patience, and industriousness are, along with courage, among those virtues of which I spoke earlier as sometimes being labelled 'self-regarding', on the grounds that an agent possessing them need not be motivated by other-regarding considerations and may exercise them entirely for his or her own benefit. They have also been thought of as 'corrective' virtues,[9] for they are seen as corrective of certain desires and feelings which may tempt us to act inappropriately or unreasonably. Thus Aquinas speaks of them as being generally concerned with the passions, and to be distinguished from one another by specifying the individual 'passion' each virtue is concerned with. Temperance, for instance, is, according to Aquinas, about the greatest pleasures of touch: meat, drink, and sex. (He regarded chastity as an aspect of temperance.) The temperate person would therefore abstain from food, drink, or sex on those occasions when it would for some reason be wrong or unwise for him or her to indulge.

If temperance is understood as corrective of a particular passion then it can perhaps best be explained in terms of the agent's behaviour on particular occasions: she acts in a temperate manner if and only if on a given occasion she sees that a certain course of action would provide her with immediate and easily accessible pleasure, and this is a reason for taking that course. But she considers whether or not in the circumstances there is an overriding reason against doing so. If she finds that there is, then she will not opt for the pleasure-yielding course. She is a temperate person if on a high proportion of relevant occasions she behaves in this manner. She may be more or less tempted by the promise of pleasure, and where she is tempted she will need some strength of will to resist the temptation and act on what she herself regards as the overriding reason. A temperate person will, at least in these respects, not be self-indulgent.[10] But nor will she err in the opposite direction and abstain when it would be foolish to do so. Temperance appears to be as Geach describes it: a humdrum, commonsense matter of being neither distracted from great ends by short-term enjoyments, nor damaging oneself by excessive abstinence.[11] But it is clear that, so understood, there is

---

[9] See e.g. Philippa Foot, 'Virtues and Vices', in *Virtues and Vices* (Oxford: Basil Blackwell, 1978). Foot discusses the thesis that in general virtues are corrective, but distinguishes between those which, like courage, correct some specific temptation, and those which, like charity, correspond to a deficiency in motivation.

[10] For this view of the 'corrective' virtues see G. Taylor and S. Wolfram, 'The Self-Regarding and the Other-Regarding Virtues', *Philosophical Quarterly* 18 (1968), sect. 3.

[11] Peter Geach, *The Virtues* (Cambridge: Cambridge University Press, 1977), ch. 7.

much this virtue takes for granted: the agent, to sort out what are and what are not good reasons for indulgence or abstinence, must have some picture in her mind of what it is worthwhile to do in her life, and must be capable of engaging in practical reasoning. It is only within this framework that virtues can operate as correctives to temptation. Even given this there still seems to be some difficulty with this view of temperance. As the case of the vicious amply demonstrated, it is only too easy to arrange the weighting of one's reasons to suit one's own inclinations and preferences, but we should hardly regard as temperate a person who always reached the conclusion that on this occasion there was no reason against her taking the immediately pleasurable course. On the contrary, she seems to be a candidate for gluttony or lust. To qualify for the virtue she has to be sincere in her evaluations; she must not, at those times when she is tempted, subordinate (for this reason) other values to that of pleasure. And now temperance is a much more far-reaching and less 'humdrum' virtue than it at first appeared. If it is still to be thought of as corrective of passion, then 'passion' now refers to more than an occurrent desire for some pleasure; it refers to everything that cannot be called specifically 'rational', and so includes perceptions and attitudes as well as desires and feelings. So interpreted, temperance, and all the other virtues of the 'self-regarding' or 'corrective' type, apply primarily not to particular actions but rather to the agent's overall perspective on life. Temperance now is concerned not merely with controlling certain desires for specific pleasures, but indicates a 'tempered' outlook on life, which requires both the harmonious interaction of all the faculties, and a balanced sense of value. Taken in this sense temperance is a general rather than a specific virtue, applicable to all the vicious and not only to a particular set of them.

The harm inherent in possession of any one of the vices affected all of a person's faculties. It is then only to be expected that the good of a countervailing virtue should be equally spread. Nor, given the overlap and connection between the vices, is it surprising that their countervailing virtues should similarly overlap and interconnect. Taking 'passion' in its widest sense the, for example, temperate person will not only be in control of her appetites; her way of perceiving the world and herself will be 'well-tempered' also. She will therefore also possess all the other corrective virtues, for she will know when it is, for instance, worthwhile to face the danger, to swallow her anger, to engage in activity rather than be idle. Having a balanced sense of value she will exercise practical wisdom in her deliberations, and this in turn entails that she will have that kind of self-esteem which was essential to self-healing. Being temperate will also include awareness of the range and limits of her powers, and this again means acknowledgement of others, of her impact on them, and theirs on her. Not being governed by wishful thought she will have a grip on reality, including the reality of the other as a person like herself. In his discussion of temperance John Casey (*Pagan Virtue*, ch. 3) thinks of it as (among other things) the virtue of human relationships. This is so because the intemperate cannot accept that anything should come between their need and its immediate gratification. This in turn will mean ignoring others and their needs. In learning to control themselves they thereby learn to respect the other. So understood, the possession of temperance will bring with it not only possession of all the virtues belonging to the 'corrective' class, but will also include at least some of the other-regarding virtues. The doctrine of the interconnection of the virtues gets much support when virtues are thought of as operating on this level.

Nevertheless, the corrective virtues can still be distinguished one from another. Aquinas, in reply to the question whether temperance is a special virtue, points out the different ways of looking at it (*ST* 2a2ae q. 141 art. 2). Temperance is a general virtue if one takes 'temperateness' to signify a certain moderation which reason applies to operations and passions; in this sense it is common to all the virtues. But there is still a difference between e.g. temperance and fortitude: the latter refers to firmness in facing danger or enduring adverse circumstances rather than to correcting appetites. The 'well-tempered' person will also have fortitude in that she will know what to face or bear and what to avoid, but what is common to the two virtues will be specifically applied in different circumstances. The way in which her basic attitudes reveal themselves on different sorts of occasions will specify the virtue.

The particularization of the virtues now is from inside out, rather than from outside in, as was initially suggested. Instead of starting from particular actions which in specific circumstances constitute the exercise of temperance, we now postulate the 'well-tempered' person and consider how she would act in given circumstances.

Particularization will have degrees: the more specifically defined, the more suitable as countervailing to a particular vice. But also the more superficial. If temperance is to be concerned specifically with the pleasures of eating and drinking, then it is corrective of gluttony only; if more generally with sensual pleasures, then of lust also. The temperate are neither gluttonous nor lustful. On the other hand, this characterization gives little indication of the fundamental wrong which, in the case of the vicious, needs to be remedied. Less specifically, temperance may be seen as a corrective of greed of all types, including greed for acknowledgement, power, applause, or self-sufficiency. The remedy here touches the more fundamental, but it now again applies to a whole range of vices.

The most profitable way of looking for specific virtues as countervailing to particular vices is to see whether, given possession of a universally applicable virtue such as self-love or temperance in its widest sense, there is among the virtuous traits this generates one which is more suited to one specific vice than to the others. So for instance, temperance seen as curbing greed is appropriately enough linked to gluttony and lust. It is not, however, a promising candidate as a virtue corrective of sloth. The greedy at least have desires and are engaged, even if unfortunately so. But this does not apply to the slothful. Casey, however, in his discussion of the topic, sees particularly sloth as a disposition that shows failure in temperance (*Pagan Virtue*, 105–10). As he says, the slothful shrink from activity; they do not see the world as something to be acted upon, and so their lives are aimless and unordered. It is true, as he suggests, that the 'well-tempered' person would not have these characteristics, but the mark peculiar to the slothful is that they do not even have the material on which aims and order could be imposed. A degree of self-love would provide them with these, for it would give them both the feeling of being alive and a sense of value. But specifically, rather than temperance it is a kind of basic courage that the slothful are in need of. The minimum correction of sloth is to be prepared to engage oneself with some aspect of the world and so to find some motivation for action. But engagement itself requires a degree of courage, if one thinks of it as resisting the temptation to take the easy way out. For it means breaking through the observer-position and making an impact on the world for which one is responsible, rather than remaining safely in one's self-circumscribed domain. Casey himself sees a possible objection to his interpretation of sloth as a form of intemperance: it tends to stress particularly the value and importance of order and discipline, thereby seemingly not taking account of other values, such as spontaneity and flexibility and imaginative playfulness. Maybe so, but such criticism does not apply to the kind of courage needed to engage and assert oneself, for *any* sort of activity is included.

The type of courage needed by the slothful is hardly that of the Homeric hero. It has nothing to do with achieving honour and nobility, but is merely the disposition to face the risks and dangers involved in engagements and the pursuit of goals. Aristotle suggests that there is a link between courage and anger (*thumos*), and this is a point which may plausibly be applied to the present context. The courageous are spirited in the face of risk or danger and 'the quasi-courage that is due to spirit seems to be the most natural, and if it includes deliberate choice and purpose it is considered to be courage'.[12]

If one thinks of what motivating force might be pumped into those with slothful dispositions then *thumos*, the spirited motivating feeling, is precisely what is needed to help them overcome that which they see as an obstacle to any engagement at all. Anger is at least a promising candidate for this role. It may be directed outwards at some person or activity in the world, or inwards, where it may focus on the agent's reluctance to engage with what he thinks worthwhile and be strong enough to sweep aside whatever the feelings are that hold him back. Even if this amounts to only 'quasi-courage', in the case of the slothful it functions as a countervailing virtue.

Anger, or in general feelings of the *thumos*-type, may, then, be linked to a type of courage and be of help to the agent in facing perceived difficulties and dangers. This suggests that a theory according to which acting virtuously is to overcome some passion is mistaken, or is at any rate far too simple.[13] Feelings tend not to operate always

---

[12] *Nicomachean Ethics*, 1116^{b}26–7. 'Natural courage' is similar to courage proper in that it leads to the relevant type of conduct; it differs from it as it lacks its fine motivation. For a discussion of the relation between courage and anger see Robert Gay, 'Courage and *Thumos*', *Philosophy* 63 (1988), 255–65. See also Casey, *Pagan Virtue*, ch. 2.

[13] Von Wright, *Varieties of Goodness*, seems to hold this view, and even to suggest that for every specifiable virtue there is some one particular passion to be overcome.

on the same side, and while some may have to be battled with, others may assist in the battle. David Pears[14] draws attention to a similar point which Aristotle seems to be making in relation to temperance. The 'subtle idea' which Pears ascribes to him hinges on Aristotle's distinction between the person who is sufficiently self-controlled to curb excessive sensual desires on the one hand, and the truly temperate on the other. Both are alike, he says, in not doing anything against reason for the sake of bodily pleasures. But the self-controlled has bad desires not experienced by the temperate, who would not feel pleasures which are contrary to reason (*Nicomachean Ethics* 1152ᵃ1–7). While both the self-controlled and the temperate share the same rational pleasure in doing what they think is right, and would be pained if they did wrong, they differ in that the self-controlled would feel pleasure if he indulged in excess, whereas the temperate person would feel lack of pleasure. But pleasure is naturally attached to the gratification of the basic appetites for food, drink, and sex, and cannot be easily and immediately shed even if perceived to interfere with rational pleasures. It could be that, in the case of the temperate, the initial pleasure had gradually died away, but, Pears suggests, it is much more plausible to take Aristotle to mean that he would experience disgust and revulsion at the thought of such indulgences. Just as feelings of anger may help an agent to face the danger, so feelings of disgust may help him to abstain from excessive indulgence. Hume makes a similar point when discussing the (in his view artificial and female) virtue of chastity: attaching shame to infidelity, Hume thinks, helps to impose 'a due constraint' on women's behaviour, but it is not quite enough, for 'the temptation is here of the strongest', and women will tend to find the means to save their reputation even when yielding to temptation. It is therefore necessary, he says, that 'there shou'd be some preceding backwardness or dread, which may prevent their first approaches, and may give the female sex a repugnance to all expressions, and postures, and liberties, that have an immediate relation to that enjoyment' (*Treatise of Human Nature* bk. 3, pt. 2, sect. 12).

In all these cases the relevant feeling has its source in some version of a universal healing virtue, for neither anger nor revulsion could

---

[14] 'Aristotle's Analysis of Courage', *Midwest Studies in Philosophy* 3 (1978), 273–85.

operate on the side of reason unless the agent had some grip on what it is more or less worthwhile for him to engage with.

The suggestion was that countervailing virtues to specific vices should be extracted from the constituents of the general virtues of genuine self-love or temperance. Such individual virtues are not character-traits the agent possesses over and above these general ones; they are merely those which are to be emphasized as being particularly applicable in a given context. But owing to the complexity of the vices this is not always a straightforward matter. So, for instance, it seemed obvious that temperance in its specific form should be the virtue controlling sensual pleasures, and hence be countervailing to gluttony and lust, and this is indeed so if the relevant vicious are thought of as indulging excessively in various forms of pleasure. It is appropriate also if the lustful are seen as greedy for power and the gluttonous as greedy for nourishment. But if in the latter case the need expressed is taken to be for human affection, then temperance seems less relevant. The glutton's desires may be 'excessive', but there may also be a genuine need which can be satisfied only by a response from others. Temperance will make him see that his desires were unreasonably demanding, and in any case will make him aware of the harm to himself if they were indulged, but in this case such insights are not enough. What is further needed appears to be again a type of courage: he needs fortitude to endure what apparently cannot be changed, and the resoluteness to deal adequately with and not be defeated by circumstances beyond his control.

A certain type of courage may also be seen as the countervailing virtue particularly suited to avarice. The avaricious are miserly, and so it may be thought that a more appropriate virtue would be liberality or generosity. But these have traditionally been defined in terms of helpfulness towards others, and so do not touch the misers' meanness towards themselves. The avaricious desire above all a guaranteed security, and their dominant state of consciousness is the anxiety that their security may be in danger. Consequently, they are suspicious of others as a possible threat. They lack all trust, and trust (or faith) itself could be suggested as the needed virtue. But trust means taking risks, for it is needed only where there is not sufficient evidence for a high degree of certainty. The avaricious see risks everywhere, all of them, apparently, not worth taking. Trust, and in particular trust in themselves, may have a role here similar to that of anger described earlier, in that it involves feelings which may operate on the side of reason: the avaricious need a feeling of confidence in themselves which is expressed in the belief that they can assess properly which risks should or should not be taken, and in appropriate action. Such confidence is required particularly in their attitude towards others, whose actions and reactions they cannot control and which therefore lack total reliability. The relevant courage, then, consists not only in the capacity to take risks, but also in being prepared to accept lack of control at certain times or in certain areas, in the recognition that being in control is here not something that can be achieved.

For the different forms of vicious pride the obvious countervailing virtues seemed to be modesty or humility. Neither appears to be a particularly promising candidate. Humility is usually understood as a specifically Christian virtue, concerned with the relation of human beings to a deity, and awareness of their insignificance from that point of view. Modesty is an unfashionable and debatable virtue. The term 'modest', in contexts where it is not applied to people, indicates the less than desirable: a modest achievement or a modest income can give satisfaction to only those whose expectations are pitched rather low. A modest person is often thought to be one who meekly submits to the opinions of her elders and betters, and herself to show no spirit of her own. It is a convenience for others, perhaps, rather than a remedy for self-harm. Hence for Nietzsche it belongs to what count as virtues in the slave-morality,[15] and Hume speaks of it as that artificial virtue which is to be instilled in women if their chastity is to be relied upon.[16] As Hume suggests, modesty is often—though not necessarily—connected with sexual behaviour. Scruton defines

---

[15] 'What is Noble?' in *Beyond Good and Evil* (cf. Goethe's drinking-song: 'Nur die Lumpen sind bescheiden'; and Schopenhauer: 'the virtue of modesty is, I suppose, a fine invention for fools and knaves', 'Aphorisms on the Wisdom of Life', in *Parerga and Paralipomena*).

[16] But it is not to be instilled in all women for, Hume says, the only demand on men is that they do not have *entire* liberty to indulge their appetites, and so, the implication is, for the convenience of men there also have to be women who lack chastity and modesty. Hume makes it quite clear that he thinks chastity and modesty very 'artificial': they are arbitrary artificial virtues and quite unlike the 'natural' artificial virtue of justice.

it as 'the disposition to feel bodily shame (including sexual shame) and so to avoid its occasion' (*Sexual Desire*, 155). He adds that 'the usual name for immodest desire—the desire which rides roughshod over the reticence of others, and treats every new object as an equivalent of the last—is lust.' Modesty on this understanding seems countervailing to lust rather than to any form of pride. But on the other hand, in their desire to establish power over another the lustful exhibit a considerable degree of arrogance, and modesty may be seen as rectifying that. The modest person does not put herself forward, she does not aim at making her importance felt by demands on others which are excessive and unjustifiable, as are constant demands for attention or flattery. But this may be merely a matter of behaviour, of outward compliance with convention. The genuinely modest person has to moderate not merely her behaviour but also her will, which does not mean that she cannot assert herself. Demands on others may after all be perfectly justifiable and indeed necessary. Modesty rather entails a balanced assessment of one's own powers and their limitations, and thereby of one's own position vis-à-vis that of others. Pride in all its forms has to do with assessing our own worth, and so it is not surprising that modesty seen as proper pride should suggest itself as countervailing to its vicious forms.

But its role is after all restricted. A modest person, feeling relatively secure in her assessment of self-worth, does not have to rely on flattery or on comparison with others to set her in a favourable light, and so modesty may be the virtue needed by the vain and the conceited. But it does not seem to touch the wholly arrogant, for in their isolating deification of themselves they do not deign to use such props for self-esteem. It is rather some version of humility which is appropriate to their case. Humility connects with modesty in that both set limits to consciousness of self, but they differ entirely in their manner of doing so.[17] Unlike modesty, humility does not balance self- and other-worth, it does not concern the relation of self to other, and does not concern self-esteem, either. It operates in a different dimension from that where vicious and proper pride oppose one another. Kant speaks of humility in comparing oneself with others as not being

[17] Cf. Nicolai Hartmann, *Ethic* (Berlin: Walter de Gruyter, 1962), ch. 53.

a duty at all; and moreover, on those occasions when it involves a degradation of one's own personality it is opposed to a duty to oneself.[18] In his view true humility 'must inevitably follow upon our sincerely and exactly comparing ourselves with the moral law (its holiness and rigour)'. Humility limits consciousness of self through an awareness of something outside and above human beings which brings home to them their contingency and lack of absoluteness. The object and nature of this reaction is of course variously understood and differs widely in its implications. For Kant the awareness was due to an understanding of the moral law and so, since as rational beings we ourselves are lawgivers, it leads to self-respect as well as respect for others, in so far as we all share a rational nature. Aquinas naturally sees humility as a Christian virtue and speaks of it as being caused by reverence for God (*ST* 2a2ae q. 161), and for Scheler it is the realization that there is something but might have been nothing.[19] But however different the views as to what it is that evokes humility, it always denotes something which symbolizes the supernatural and more than human, by comparison with which individuals feel themselves to be limited and dependent. Humility is always linked with a certain type of feeling, usually called 'reverence' ('Achtung' in Kant). The connection is a conceptual one in that both the awareness and the relevant feeling are constituent of humility; the reverential reaction is part of the virtue. Reverence itself is a complex phenomenon, implying a sense of wonder as well as of unease and fear, and feelings such as these are clearly countervailing to the arrogantly prouds' cultivation of their godlike self-image.

Quite different from that of the proud is the problem of the envious and the resentful. Being grudging and revengeful towards others, a virtue implying a change of attitude in this respect would seem to be appropriate. Some form of generosity suggests itself, though not of the usual kind, which involves giving to others because the agent perceives in them a primarily material need for what he is able to give. James D. Wallace makes a here relevant distinction between

[18] *Metaphysics of Morals*, pt. II; *Metaphysical Principles of Virtue*, pt. I; *Elements of Ethics*, pt. I, ch. 2, para. 11.

[19] *Vom Umsturz der Werte* (1955), referred to by Francis Dunlop, *Scheler* (London: Claridge, 1991).

'economic generosity' and 'generous-mindedness'.[20] Of the latter he says that it has to do with making judgements about the merits and failings of other people, and a generous-minded person is one who wants to think well of others. This is indeed an attitude the envious and resentful lack and need, for, as Wallace says, it may counteract an inclination to build oneself up by tearing others down. From the point of view of the envious or resentful they either have to cease seeing others as a source of harm and suspicion, or they must be prepared to forgive them for having done or intending to do whatever is thought to be damaging. Even if the perception of harm is groundless and unreasonable, a genuine act of forgiveness is an act of charity expressing trust in the other in spite of having supposedly been capable of causing injury. Perhaps the countervailing virtue should be called 'magnanimity' rather than 'generosity'.[21] Trust being a positive response to others in conditions of risk, there can be little or no evidence that it will be rewarded by an equally positive response, little or no evidence that others will not return evil for good. To trust is to cast one's bread upon the waters. The trusting person does not judge others or first look for evidence to show that they are indeed trustworthy, but simply accepts them as fellow human beings. There are no doubt dangers in such an attitude, but any constraints which it may seem necessary for the sake of prudence to impose upon an attitude of trust will not alter the position of magnanimity as countervailing to envy and resentment.

Kolnai says of the trust involved in genuine forgiveness that it may be looked upon 'not to be sure as the starting-point and the very basis, but perhaps as the epitome and culmination of morality'.[22] He seems to think of such trust as both the gist of morality, and also an ideal rarely if ever achieved. An individual having that trust which is the culmination of morality would presumably be a saint, a holy fool, perhaps, whose optimism and faith in human nature survive what would normally be regarded as sufficient counter-evidence and

---

[20] James D. Wallace, *Virtues and Vices* (Ithaca, NY: Cornell University Press, 1978), ch. 5. In his view the parallels are not exact, and 'generosity' is used metaphorically in 'generous-mindedness'.

[21] Aurel Kolnai, in 'Forgiveness', *Proceedings of the Aristotelean Society* (1973–4), discusses the distinction between cases of genuine and semblance forgiveness.

[22] Ibid. 105.

reasonable grounds for caution and suspicion.[23] Trust of this sort, whether holy or foolish, clearly goes beyond the requirements for countervailing virtues. More directly relevant is Kolnai's reference to trust as the epitome of morality. In a more mundane form[24] it has made its appearance in connection with a number of the particular virtues discussed. It is a feature of the kinds of courage suggested as countervailing to sloth, avarice, and gluttony, as well as needed by the envious and resentful. It can also be seen as countervailing to pride (and to lust, if the lustful are thought of as being extremely arrogant in their attitude towards and treatment of others). A degree of trust is implied by the virtue of justice. Justice is a social virtue in the sense that it is a practice meant to serve the community as a whole, the expectation being that everyone is to have his or her 'fair' share, and everyone's rights are to be respected. Such expectations depend for their approximate fulfilment on a measure of support from members of the given society. The existence and continuation of the practice being dependent on co-operation and reciprocity, thinking and acting justly demands a considerable degree of trust in the virtue of others and in the viability of aiming at a common good. Philippa Foot classes justice with charity as a 'virtue of attachment' which, rather than designed to keep in check some particular desire or tendency, corresponds to a deficiency of motivation in that we tend not to care much for the rights of others, in contrast to the attachment which we have for our own.[25] A just person is concerned about the rights of others, sufficiently so to act accordingly on relevant occasions. The proud are prominent among the vicious who pay no attention to the rights of others, and a sense of justice would evidently rectify this. So justice and the trust it involves may be proposed as another countervailing virtue to pride in particular.

The function of the countervailing virtues was to heal that which the vices corrupted. Since individual virtues are, like the vices, interconnected, there was some (limited) choice as to which virtuous

---

[23] Annette Baier asks: 'Are virtues ways of shutting one's eyes to danger, seeing the good not the bad prospects? Maybe they are.' 'Theory and Reflective Practices', *Postures of the Mind* (London: Methuen, 1985), 220.

[24] More mundane from an outsider's point of view. For someone who has to fight off feelings of anxiety, envy, or resentment it may well appear to be a saintly virtue.

[25] Foot, *Virtues and Vices*, 9.

traits to emphasize as being either generally or specifically the most appropriate ones. Similarly, what precisely the 'healing' consists in may be approached in a variety of ways, and any feature picked out will inevitably connect with others. Traditionally the model for the virtuous has been that in their case reason is in control, and since the vicious discussed in earlier chapters were characterized as being irrational, rationality may be selected as one of the prominent features of the virtues here introduced.

To speak of rationality as prominent may suggest the picture of the virtues as curbing the passions when these incite us to act against reason, and so to think of them as being primarily a matter of controlling the passions and exercising strength of will.[26] Self-control, on such a view, is the supreme virtue, rather than merely one among many others. But this hardly goes to the heart of the matter. The irrationality of the vicious affected all their faculties, and the rationality of the virtuous should be similarly comprehensive. The difference between them is in their overall attitude towards themselves and the world, and in the nature of what engages and attaches them. The irrationality and rationality of, respectively, vices and virtues do not concern the relation between 'passion' and 'reason'; they refer rather to the complex of cognitive, affective, and volitional dispositions and states involved in the attitude and direction of caring.[27] For the vicious the focus of care was exclusively their own position, and the irrationality of their attitude was in its lack of cohesion and consequent deception of self. Conversely, the rationality of that of the virtuous contributes to their authenticity. This is so because they do not live in a fantasy world which can be kept going only by distortion and suppression of desires, a process which leaves the agent at their mercy and robs him of control over his life. Rational caring is a move against self-centredness. The carer is not necessarily

---

[26] E.g. von Wright: 'He (the man of virtue) has learnt to conquer the obscuring effects of passion upon his judgments of good and evil.' And: 'The various forms of virtues, it may be said, are so many forms of self-control.' (*Varieties of Goodness*, 147 and 149.)

[27] The points about caring are raised by Harry Frankfurt, 'The Importance of What We Care About' and 'Identification and Wholeheartedness', in *The Importance of What We Care About* (Cambridge: Cambridge University Press, 1988). See also Baier, 'Caring about Caring: A Reply to Frankfurt', *Postures of the Mind*, 93–108.

altruistic, but his attention and concern is outward-directed, away from himself and his status and towards either others or activities and causes he engages with. Such attachments will of course make him vulnerable and require the kinds of courage earlier referred to. Nevertheless, they are liberating, for it is no longer constant care for his own position and its attending anxieties which govern the agent's view of the world, but it is the characteristics of the objects of his care which are its main influence. So directed caring offers an escape from the narrow and paralysing world of wholly explicit self-consciousness to at least occasional self-forgetfulness. 'Liberation' implies a degree of regained control over one's life. This does not mean that caring is a matter of the will in the sense that one can simply decide or make up one's mind what to care about. Decisions may have some part to play in the process, but caring for something involves emotional commitments which cannot be produced on order. Caring is not in this sense voluntary, but nor is it an occurrence quite passively experienced; something can usually be done to assist its cultivation. Most importantly, a wholehearted commitment to what one cares about means that, although not directly under the agent's control, caring nonetheless engages the will in that the agent willingly identifies and takes responsibility for relevant feelings, attitudes, and actions.

BIBLIOGRAPHY

ANNAS, JULIA, *The Morality of Happiness* (Oxford: Oxford University Press, 1993).

AQUINAS, THOMAS, *Summa Theologiae*, parts 1a2ae and 2a2ae.

ARISTOTLE, *Nicomachean Ethics*.

ARMON-JONES, CLAIRE, *Varieties of Affect* (Hemel Hempstead: Harvester Wheatsheaf, 1991).

AUDEN, W. H., *The Dyer's Hand and Other Essays* (New York: Random House, 1956).

——*Seven Deadly Sins* (London: Sunday Times Publications, 1962).

BAIER, ANNETTE, *Postures of the Mind* (London: Methuen, 1985).

BALZAC, HONORÉ DE, *Cousin Bette* (Harmondsworth: Penguin, 1965).

——*Cousin Pons* (Harmondsworth: Penguin, 1978).

BRADLEY, A. C., 'The Rejection of Falstaff', in G. K. Hurter (ed.), *King Henry IV Parts 1 and 2*, Casebook Studies (London: Macmillan, 1970).

BRADLEY, F. H., *Ethical Studies* (Oxford: Oxford University Press, 1962).

BROCKMAN, B. A. (ed.), *Shakespeare: Coriolanus*, Casebook Series (London: Macmillan 1977).

CASEY, JOHN, *Pagan Virtue* (Oxford: Oxford University Press, 1990).

CAVELL, STANLEY, *Disowning Knowledge in Six Plays of Shakespeare* (Cambridge: Cambridge University Press, 1987).

COTTINGHAM, JOHN, 'Partiality and the Virtues', in R. Crisp (ed.), *How Should One Live?* (Oxford: Oxford University Press, 1996).

CRISP, ROGER (ed.), *How Should One Live? Essays on the Virtues* (Oxford: Oxford University Press, 1996).

DESCARTES, RENÉ, *Passions of the Soul*.

DILLON, ROBIN S. (ed.), *Dignity, Character and Self-Respect* (New York: Routledge, 1995).

DUNLOP, FRANCIS, *Scheler* (London: Claridge, 1991).

FINGARETTE, HERBERT, *Self-Deception* (London: Routledge and Kegan Paul, 1977).

FOOT, PHILIPPA, *Virtues and Vices* (Oxford: Basil Blackwell, 1978).

——*Natural Goodness* (Oxford: Clarendon, 2001).

FRANK, DANIEL H., 'Anger as a Vice: A Maimonidean Critique of Aristotle's Ethics', *History of Philosophy Quarterly* 7 (1990), 269–81.

FRANKFURT, HARRY, 'Identification and Wholeheartedness', in Ferdinand Schoeman (ed.), *Responsibility, Character and the Emotions* (Cambridge: Cambridge University Press, 1987).

—— *The Importance of What We Care About* (Cambridge: Cambridge University Press, 1988).

FREUD, SIGMUND, *Three Essays on the Theory of Sexuality*.

FUKUYAMA, FRANCIS, *The End of History and the Last Man* (Harmondsworth: Penguin, 1992).

GAITA, RAIMOND (ed.), *Value and Understanding: Festschrift in Honour of Peter Winch* (London: Routledge, 1990).

GAY, ROBERT, 'Courage and *Thumos*', *Philosophy* 63 (1988), 255–65.

GLOVER, JONATHAN, *I: The Philosophy and Psychology of Personal Identity* (Harmondsworth: Penguin, 1988).

GOLDTHORPE, RHIANNON, *Sartre: Literature and Theory* (Cambridge: Cambridge University Press, 1984).

GREENSPAN, PATRICIA, *Emotions and Reasons* (New York: Routledge, 1988).

HARRÉ, ROM, *Personal Being* (Oxford: Basil Blackwell, 1983).

HARTMANN, NICOLAI, *Ethic* (Berlin: Walter de Gruyter, 1962).

HUME, DAVID, *A Treatise of Human Nature*, books II and III.

HURSTHOUSE, ROSALIND, *On Virtue Ethics* (Oxford: Clarendon, 1999).

—— LAWRENCE, G., and QUINN, W. (eds.), *Virtues and Reasons: Essays in Honour of Philippa Foot* (Oxford: Clarendon, 1995).

INGHAM, PATRICIA, *Dickens, Women and Language* (Toronto: University of Toronto Press, 1992).

KANT, IMMANUEL, *The Metaphysics of Morals*.

—— *Lectures on Ethics*.

—— *Metaphysical First Principles of the Doctrine of Virtue*, tr. Mary Gregor (Cambridge: Cambridge University Press, 1993).

KENNY, ANTHONY, *Action, Emotion and Will* (London: Routledge and Kegan Paul, 1963).

KIERKEGAARD, SØREN, *Either/Or*.

KOLNAI, AUREL, 'Forgiveness', *Proceedings of the Aristotelean Society* (1973–4), 91–106.

LAWRENCE, GAVIN, 'The Rationality of Morality', in R. Hursthouse, G. Lawrence, and W. Quinn (eds.), *Virtues and Reasons: Essays in Honour of Philippa Foot* (Oxford: Clarendon, 1995).

McGINN, COLIN, *The Character of Mind* (Oxford: Oxford University Press, 1982).

MacINTYRE, A., *After Virtue* (London: Duckworth, 1981).

McLAUGHLIN, BRIAN, and RORTY, A. OKSENBERG (eds.), *Perspective on Self-Deception* (Berkeley: University of California Press, 1988).

MILL, JOHN STUART, *Utilitarianism*.

MISCHEL, THEODORE (ed.), *The Self* (Oxford: Basil Blackwell, 1977).

MONTAIGNE, MICHEL DE, *Essays* (Harmondsworth: Penguin, 1958).

MONTEFIORE, ALAN, 'Self-Reality, Self-Respect, and Respect for Others', *Midwest Studies in Philosophy* 3 (1978), 195–208.

MURDOCH, IRIS, *The Sovereignty of Good* (London: Routledge and Kegan Paul, 1970).

NAGEL, THOMAS, *Mortal Questions* (Cambridge: Cambridge University Press, 1979).

NIETZSCHE, FRIEDRICH, *On the Genealogy of Morals*.

——— *Beyond Good and Evil*.

NOZICK, ROBERT, *Anarchy, State and Utopia* (Oxford: Basil Blackwell, 1974).

NUSSBAUM, MARTHA, *The Fragility of Goodness* (Cambridge: Cambridge University Press, 1986).

PEARS, DAVID, 'Aristotle's Analysis of Courage', *Midwest Studies in Philosophy* 3 (1978), 273–85.

RAWLS, JOHN, *A Theory of Justice* (Oxford: Oxford University Press, 1973).

REID, THOMAS, *Essays on the Active Powers of the Human Mind*.

SARTRE, JEAN-PAUL, *Being and Nothingness*, tr. Hazel E. Barnes (London: Methuen, 1981).

——— *In Camera*, tr. Stuart Gilbert (London: Penguin, 1988).

SCHELER, MAX, *Ressentiment*, tr. W. W. Holdheim (New York: Schocken, 1972).

——— *The Nature of Sympathy* (London: Routledge and Kegan Paul, 1979).

SCHOEMAN, FERDINAND (ed.), *Responsibility, Character and the Emotions* (Cambridge: Cambridge University Press, 1987).

SCHOPENHAUER, ARTUR, *Parerga and Paralipomena*.

SCRUTON, ROGER, *Sexual Desire* (London: Weidenfeld and Nicolson, 1986).

SHKLAR, JUDITH, *Ordinary Vices* (Cambridge, Mass.: Harvard University Press, 1984).

SOLOMON, ROBERT C., 'The Virtue of Love', *Midwest Studies in Philosophy* 13, *Ethical Theory, Character and Virtue* (1988), 12–31.

STOCKER, MICHAEL, 'Psychic Feelings', *Australasian Journal of Philosophy* 61/1 (March 1983), 5–26.

STRAWSON, P. F., *Freedom and Resentment and Other Essays* (London: Methuen, 1980).

TAYLOR, CHARLES, *Sources of the Self* (Cambridge: Cambridge University Press, 1989).

TAYLOR, GABRIELE, *Pride, Shame, and Guilt* (Oxford: Oxford University Press, 1985).

—— 'Envy and Jealousy', *Midwest Studies in Philosophy* 13 (1988), 233–49.

TAYLOR, GABRIELE, 'Deadly Vices?', in R. Crisp (ed.), *How Should One Live?* (Oxford: Oxford University Press, 1996).

—— 'Vices and the Self', in A. Phillips Griffiths (ed.), *Philosophy, Psychology and Psychiatry* (Cambridge: Cambridge University Press, 1994).

—— and WOLFRAM, S., 'The Self-Regarding and the Other-Regarding Virtues', *Philosophical Quarterly* 18 (1968), 238–48.

VON WRIGHT, G. H., *The Varieties of Goodness* (London: Routledge and Kegan Paul, 1953).

WALLACE, JAMES D., *Virtues and Vices* (Ithaca, NY: Cornell University Press, 1978).

WENZEL, S., *The Sin of Sloth: Acedia in Medieval Thought and Literature* (Chapel Hill: University of North Carolina, 1967).

WIGGINS, DAVID, *Needs, Values, Truth* (Oxford: Basil Blackwell, 1987).

WILLIAMS, BERNARD, *Problems of the Self* (Cambridge: Cambridge University Press, 1973).

—— *Moral Luck* (Cambridge: Cambridge University Press, 1981).

—— *Ethics and the Limits of Philosophy* (London: Fontana, 1985).

WOLLHEIM, RICHARD, *The Thread of Life* (Cambridge: Cambridge University Press, 1984).

INDEX